Betrayed and Rejected

Betrayed AND REJECTED

The Story Behind The
BERGHOLZ AMISH HAIR CUTTINGS

Linda Shrock

Copyright 2021 Linda Shrock

All rights reserved. No part of this book may be reproduced or transmitted in any form or by any means, electronic or mechanical, including photocopying and recording, or by any information storage or retrieval system, without permission in writing from the publisher or author.

The names of individuals and family members have been changed to protect their identities and their privacy.

ISBN-13 (paperback): 978-1-943496-21-1

Front cover design: Josh Aul, Nexlevel Design, LLC, www.nexleveldesign.com
Editor snd interior layout: Kara Starcher

Published in Association with Total Fusion Press, Strasburg, OH
www.totalfusionpress.com

30 29 28 27 26 25 24 23 22 21   1 2 3 4 5

Contents

Introduction 1

Part One: Memories

1 Childhood 7
2 Fredericktown 20
3 Home Life 29

Part Two: The Meeting

4 Sixteen 41
5 Seventeen 46
6 Decisions 52
7 Disagreement 61
8 The Start 72

Part Three: Bergholz

9 The Community 83

10 Trouble Begins	88
11 The Devil	92
12 Confessions	97
13 Punishment	109

Part Four: Separations

14 Amish Prison	117
15 Haircuts	123
16 More Separation	129
17 Visions	137

Part Five: Rejection

18 More Visions	143
19 Leaving	152
20 Trouble	158
21 First Cuttings	167
22 More Attacks	170
23 Arrest	174

About the Author ... 179

Introduction

August 6, 2014
Federal Correctional Institution, Waseca • Waseca, Minnesota

AS I SIT HERE ON a hard metal chair in my lonely prison room, my thoughts go back to my childhood in Ohio, and I wonder how in the world I got myself into such a tragic mess.

I am Linda S. Mullet, daughter of Simon and Susie (Miller) Mullet. My birth certificate says my name is Malinda, but everyone calls me Linda. I was born and raised Amish in Middlefield, Geauga County, Ohio. I have nine brothers and eight sisters! Yes, you read that correctly—we had eighteen children in our family!

As I begin with my story, let me introduce you to my dad, Simon. I never heard him apologize for anything. He just made excuses or claimed he did it for a reason. Everything he did, he always said, "God told me to do _____" or "God told me to think _____." Then he would say, "If you don't like it or agree with it, leave me." My story is about the damage done to others when a person never admits mistakes or wrongdoings.

I do not have any good memories of Dad and Mom together getting along and having fun. They were always fighting and arguing. My mom's favorite songs were "If Teardrops were Pennies" (and heartaches were gold, I'd have all the riches) and "Your Cheatin' Heart." She sang those songs often. She told us girls that one day we would understand why she sang them. If my parents did get a chance to sit down on their rockers at the same time, they just sat there saying nothing or Dad was reading the papers. They argued a lot, mostly about money and paying bills. Whenever I heard loud noises, I went outside or hid in my room—I felt alone so many times.

When I was young, I heard many of my dad's conversations with family and friends. His conversations were about the devil, a lot. He read stories about the devil and told us stories about him. I was always scared. I just knew this devil was a bad man. I remember lots of times when my dad would visit his dad and mom. Their conversations were never good. I heard Grandpa Mullet say many times to my dad that he shouldn't talk like that.

As a child, I respected my dad because he was my father and the only person I knew besides my mom. As I grew older, I realized Dad was different from everyone else. It affected our school life, our young folk life, and later on, our marriages. The only thing I can think of for why he acted the way he did was he did not want his girls to be with other boys. It caused a lot of problems. Looking back, I think he was jealous of us or overly protective.

Introduction

Our family visited English people a lot and we kids would play together. The only difference was our dress and speech. Otherwise, we were just kids. When we had lunch with Englishers, the head of the house always prayed out loud for food and fellowship. That stuck with me because Amish people bow their heads and say silent prayers.

Most churches in the Amish community are just churches. Each community has its own rules to go by. I will not judge any Amish or disrespect them, so if their church rules are what they want and agree with, good for them. It's not for me. Those man-made rules are too confusing.

Part One
Memories

Childhood

OUR FAMILY LIVED ON A mini farm next to Grandfather and Grandmother Mullet and my aunts and uncles. I spent more time on Grandfather's farm than I did at home. My grandfather was farming from the time I was old enough to know and realize what was going on in this world. He owned milking cows and calves, horses, pigs, and chickens. The only animal my dad owned was a horse, and later, a pony. I helped take care of Grandfather's animals by putting straw down for bedding and hay down for food. I also helped get the animals ready for the next day. I milked my first cow when I was six years old. It was scary, but fun!

Even as young children, we could easily walk to Grandfather's farm across the field. We did not have to walk on the road. Although the road was a backcountry type of road with little traffic, Mom still told us to stay off the road. However, I have a very scary memory of the time my sister Maggie and I walked up to the back field from our pasture, not knowing that Grandfather Mullet had his herd of cows and his bull in the field. We were walking along when we noticed the cows with the bull. My dad who was cutting hay nearby yelled, "Run, girls! Run for the fence!" Too late! The bull had seen us. We ran as fast as we could. Just as I rolled under the fence, the bull was there, and bawl he did! We were two frightened little girls. Dad told us to go home and stay there, and we did.

On my days not on the farm, I played with my doll baby that I treasured dearly. I had lots of imagination and played by myself quite a bit. I would go to town or visit neighbors with a buggy and a make-believe horse. Our entryway was my house, and I stored my doll things in a clothes cupboard.

My mother managed and cared for our family's needs. She was entitled to sell Tupperware, so sometimes we walked several miles to our neighbors' homes so she could make a sale. Mom also baked at times. I remember helping package cookies for the school sale at the beginning of each school term. (The earnings from the sale were a donation for the school.) I would place a dozen cookies on a piece of cardboard and wrap it with plastic wrap. Sometimes we helped Mommy in the garden. She always had a row of burning bush trees in her garden.

Another memory from my childhood is of Dad mowing the hay down with a huge mower and letting it dry in the sun. After it dried for a couple of days, Dad would take a tedder machine and ride up and down the fields kicking the hay around to finish drying it out. When the hay was dry, Dad used a rake to make rows

Memories

Part of Grandfather and Grandmother Mullet's farm. I started milking cows in that barn.

around the field. Next, we hitched the horses, two as a team, to a huge wagon with a hay loader dragging behind the wagon. Hay came up the loader and onto the wagon. Then someone on the wagon used forks to guide the hay level on the wagon.

Once the wagon was full, we unhitched the loader and drove to the barn where there was a huge fork hanging by a rope from the beams of the barn. We fastened the fork to the hay and hitched one horse to the other end of the rope. That horse pulled the fork all the way up to the roof of the barn. Then someone inside the barn pulled a little rope to release the loose hay into the hayloft. And there it was!

When we washed clothes, we had washing machines with gasoline motors. We'd put the clothes through the wringer to press the wash water out. Then we rinsed them and put them through the wringer again. Next, we hung the wash with clothespins out on the lines to dry which took two to three hours. After they were dry, we took them down, put the pins in a basket, and carried the clothes in the house to fold, sort, and put in piles. Each pile went in the drawers in the children's room. Usually, we had one drawer for all socks and hankies. One day I went to get the wash off the line and a huge bee stung my belly. I lay on the couch the rest of the day.

We lived in a cellar house until Dad could start building the house we would live in. We all had the measles bad while living in the cellar before our new house was built. Then, Dad started building on top of our cellar house, so we moved into a little barn on our farm and slept in the hayloft. Lots of other men came to help build the house. Sometimes the men and their families stayed to visit and play cards late into the night. One night most of us children were sick and vomited all night. Dad was very tired because of getting up so often with us. Uncle Fredrick was there, and he forced all of us to say good morning, whether we wanted to or not! He was a fun, loving uncle.

Sometimes we visited Grandpa and Grandma Miller in West Farmington. These trips were always fun, but different, because my grandparents were more modern and didn't have a farm. Their house was almost on the road, a busy road. Grandpa shoed horses, so there were always lots of people coming and going. Grandpa Miller's house had a nice playroom in the pump house that we would play in. The room had little dishes, tables, a sink, and a broom and dustpan.

One time we had a Christmas gathering at Uncle David and

Memories

The brown building is the small barn we lived in while Dad built the house. This house is where I lived as a child in Middlefield, Ohio.

Grandpa and Grandma Miller's house where my mother lived as a girl.

Irene Miller's home and we received doll babies as our presents. They had no face, so Grandpa Miller said, "Here, give me your new doll." I gave the doll to him and watched as he took a pen and drew a face on my doll. He handed it back to me and said, "You don't need to be different." He was more modern and felt sorry for us that we were different.

Sometimes we had reunions with many, many people from New York and Punxsutawney, PA. We would gather underneath a huge weeping willow tree in Grandpa and Grandma Miller's yard where rows of benches and chairs were set up for us to sit on under the tree. Those days were interesting.

I remember Uncle Fredrick and my aunts Edith, Ruby, and Anna the most. I have lots and lots of cousins, too. My youngest aunt, Betsy, had Down syndrome, and I was afraid of her. She was always laughing and talking, but I couldn't understand her. She died on March 4, 1970, and Grandfather was so sad. I remember seeing him with a hanky over his face, and it made me cry.

Whenever Dad and Mom needed to leave, Aunt Nora or Aunt Wanda came to babysit us. Nora always read books and made popcorn balls. She would eat the rough part off the popcorn balls until she had a little bowl with teeny lil' balls. I asked her what they were for, and she said they were for birds like me, so I ate them!

Sundays

We went to church every two weeks. People took turns opening their houses for church because we didn't have a church building. Church lasted all day with the actual church service ending around noon. For our meal, we always had cookies, bread, and soup made in big iron kettles. During the afternoons, we played games, and in the evenings, we would sing and then go home.

Every fall and every spring was communion or "Ordnung" service. After the church service ended around noon, the children were sent outside to play while the rest of the church people who were baptized and accepted as members stayed seated. The bishop then read off the Ordnung (Amish rules) of the church. When he finished, the ministers asked each member if they agreed with the rules. If they did, those members prepared themselves to go to communion the next Sunday. Communion was held after services. The members took bread and wine as a sacrifice to forgive all their sins up to that point in life. At the end of the service, members washed each other's feet like Jesus did for the apostles. Wash feet, shake hands, and kiss to seal the membership—that's the Amish way.

On our Sundays at home, we would go for a walk, play in the creek behind our pasture, or ride ponies. Babe, a big white pony with brown spots, was my first pony. I couldn't guide her because she had a mind of her own. Sometimes I sat on her back and cried until someone came and rescued me. The first time I drove her in the cart, she went into the barn and two wheels stuck by the one-man door. I cried . . . again! She even ate my dad's newly planted trees. Eventually, I learned how to handle Babe. We also had a black pony named Indy whom I would ride flat out as fast as he could go. It was fun!

One day my sister Maggie and I went riding, and we got mad for some reason and started calling each other names. It ended when I called her "Snake!" She didn't keep her mouth shut and told Dad, so I received my first "whooping" that I remember which put "a little wall" between us. The next incident: she would wet the bed and blame it on me! When she saw that it didn't work, she made me promise to not tell on her. My sister Maggie was very self-conscious about herself.

When I was seven years old, we children were taking turns riding a pony around the corn crib. Every time I went on the other side where no one else could see, a mean-faced white puppy came out and scared me! I was frightened so badly. Finally, I said something, but no one else saw him . . . only me. I was so upset. I quit, went into the house, and told Mom about the puppy. She said I should listen to Dad and keep my cap strings tied at all times! The Amish people's rule is to keep your head covering strings always tied. It was considered modern if you left them hanging. (We had a bad habit of not tying them.) Of course, after this, I did. To me, that puppy meant never sin, don't smoke (smoking was very common on both sides of our families), don't say bad words, never listen to music, never have anything with electricity or a phone, and other things like that. If I happened to be with someone who played music, I shut my ears on purpose so I couldn't hear the words.

School Days

Amish school starts with first grade and goes to eighth grade.

They do not have kindergarten. I was good at school, but after I finished, I soon forgot the lessons.

I started school when I was six years old. My Aunt Bertha was my teacher. Dad went with us about a mile and a half from home to the schoolhouse. After he left, I cried because it was the first time I was left somewhere without Dad or Mom staying with me. I felt all alone. But some of my friends that I played with at church on Sundays were also in school, so I just played with them. I decided being left at school wasn't so bad. I spent a lot of time with Nicholas Miller, who was in my grade. Karen Miller, Miriam Miller, Donny Miller, Bonnie Fisher, Oliver Miller, and Benny Miller were other kids that I remember the most. I was a tomboy and I played better with boys than I did with girls. Why? I have no clue.

In the winter, we skated beside the school pasture. I learned to skate when I was seven or eight years old. The first time I tried, I fell back on my head. Ouch! But I got back up and skated. Since we had a hill to and from school—either way!—we took our sleds and rode down the hills. We had lots of fun! On Saturday afternoons, we would hitch up the pony and go "train sledding." We tied sled after sled together behind the pony and let it pull us in the fields. We'd ride until we were cold.

My favorite game was baseball. When I played ball, I had a bad habit of throwing my bat, so I needed to be punished for it, so I quit! I also had a bad habit of running up and down the stairs, so I had to write "I won't run again" 100 times.

Second grade was pretty much the same. My teacher at River Valley was Cecelia Miller, and the same kids from first grade were

The schoolhouse where I attended school until the end of fourth grade.

in my class. In third grade, our one-room school had a curtain through the middle, and we had two new teachers: Eli Fisher and his daughter Rachel. Rachel taught first through fourth grades and Eli taught fifth through eighth grades.

I was now with the bigger school chums. Isaac and Martin Miller sat next to me. One day I wrote a mean note about my teacher because my arm would get tired from holding it up for so long. I wrote that the teacher didn't like me and that he was mean for making me hold my arm up so long. I laid the note on my desk and was going to give it to my friend at recess. Isaac saw the note and grabbed it and read it. I was angry. He kept the note and gave it to my teacher! I had to stay in at recess and then go to the furnace room with Teacher Eli. He gave me a good lecture and explained that he was doing his best and I must not be impatient with him.

In fourth grade, we had a Christmas program, and all the

children were assigned a job except me. So, Teacher Eli said that I could be the messenger and make a speech on what was going to happen next. The play was about children going to Grandma and Grandpa's house for Christmas. The boys dressed up as married men and the girls dressed as women. They were coupled up and the lower grade kids were dressed up as children for families. They brought popcorn balls and lots of candies to Grandpa's house for the visit.

After a while, Matthew Miller and Aunt Bertha, my first-grade teacher, married each other. On their wedding day, at the reception, I asked to sit with them to eat in their corner. Aunt Bertha said yes, so I sat between them and had lots of good food and candy, not knowing that years later I would stand between them and some of their children. God's ways are not our ways. Very strange things happened.

Summertime

One summer day while we were swinging high on a swing that had a seat on each side, my sister Maggie wanted to stop really fast. She stuck her leg under the seat, and STOP we did. The force broke her leg! She had to go to the doctor to have a cast put on it.

Summer days were scorching hot, and one day Dad decided to have some fun with us children. He filled the water trough and took turns dunking us in the water and then letting us run. Meanwhile, Mom was inside looking out through the window and laughing so hard that she was crying! We were having gorgeous fun!

Another time, we had a bad rainstorm, and the creek on our property swelled up. Mom took my sisters Maggie and Mae and me wading in the creek. We waded up to our waists with our dresses on.

Family and Friends

Whenever one of us had a birthday, we'd get a gift from Grandmother Mullet and a free spanking from Uncle Boyd. Never fail, Uncle Boyd always remembered. Some days we visited Uncle Boyd's in Parkman, Ohio. On one side of his house was a lake, and we would sit in the yard watching boats with skiers. Every time a skier sank, I cried. I didn't want them to drown. But the skier always popped back up! In Uncle Boyd's woods, he had a treehouse we played in. It was beautiful and made with trees, railing and all.

One night we were at Uncle Boyd's house late and, uh-oh, Dad had no lights on his buggy to use to drive home! We started home, but lo and behold, here came a police car. Dad cut across a very bumpy field in the dark, but we made it home. (In later years, Uncle Boyd and his wife started fighting, and eventually, Boyd left his wife, Edna, and five children and went into the world. I never found out why he left.)

Another friend of my dad's whom we visited quite a bit was Nathan Fishers. Their daughter Rebecca and I were friends for a long time, and we played doll baby together. One Sunday while we were there, we children went to the woods to play. We heard someone shooting. The oldest of Nathan's boys went to check it out. He came back and said they had a "man" made of wood for a target and were practicing on him! We left the woods pretty fast! Whether what he said was true or not, I have no clue.

I remember visiting every now and then an Englisher named Kenney and his family. They visited us, too. I remember that they had rye bread, which did not taste good to me. Kenney and his wife had a son we played with named Norman. One day he came by with a broken leg. It's funny the things we remember from our childhoods.

Another time, I asked Mom if I could spend the night with my friends Rita and Mary Miller. She asked Dad and he said yes, but he told me not to leave their farm. After we were there for a while, the children hitched up their pony cart and put pressure on me: "Your dad won't know. Let's go for a ride!" Finally, I gave in, and down the road we went. Along came a buggy up the road toward us. Who should it be, but my dad. I was scolded: "Go back where you were told to go and stay there!"

I was always an outgoing, adventuresome girl. I loved to explore the ways of other people and other ways of doing things. I was open-minded and open-hearted. As a little girl, I had an instinct inside me that admired the English ways. I wondered about Englishers and watched them closely. Something pulled me toward them—a puzzle my life would explain in later years.

– 2 –

Fredericktown

ONE DAY, DAD DECIDED THINGS were not what he wanted anymore. He wanted a better life for his children compared to what he and Mom had. Geauga County had "bed courtship" and parties, plus drinking and smoking Sunday nights and at weddings. Dad did not like this. So, Dad and Mom asked Uncle Edward and his wife Susan to come to our house and stay with us while my parents went to Fredericktown, Ohio, to look for a better church. I was ten years old and in fifth grade at the time.

When Dad and Mom came back, we children were in tears. While they were gone, Susan had made a cake with fluffy white frosting and didn't let us have a piece. But after we went to bed, I had to go back downstairs for the bathroom, and Edward and Susan both had a big piece of cake! I cried. I had always loved cake, and I still do.

On April 20, 1977, we moved to the farm my parents purchased in Fredericktown, Ohio. The settlement was just starting and had only seven families when we moved there. To us, the people looked ugly, and we cried and cried all day on our moving day. One woman tried to talk to us, but she only made it worse. Finally, at night when everyone had left, we started walking around and exploring more. Even as children, we recognized lots of work had to be done. And thus, our new life began. It seemed like the whole world changed.

Not long after we moved, I met a boy who stole my heart—William Schlabach, son of Frank and Elizabeth Schlabach. William was four months older than I was, and we played together all the time and shared a lot of the same interests. By the time school started, the settlement had grown, and William attended another school, so we barely saw each other.

We had to drive five miles to school every day, morning and night, while most of the other kids walked to school. My oldest sister Maggie was our driver, and we had a palomino horse named Dick.

Our school was behind a gate on the Brenneman's property. Since most of the kids hurried off at the end of the day and we had to hitch up the horse, we usually closed the gate as we left. Sometimes others were kind and waited to close the gate after us. Edward Raber, an eighth grader, usually helped, if anybody did. His brother, Raymond, a redhead, was mean. He would kindly come in the morning and help us unhitch our horse until we found out why. He was only friendly so he could mix up the harness so it would take us longer to hitch up at night. When we figured it out, we got smart. If he came by in the morning, we would chase him off—"Go away, meanie!" He would walk away laughing.

One night on the way home from school, a huge black dog attacked our horse and buggy! He jumped up on the horse's head and bit him until blood oozed all over. I thought about jumping out of the buggy so the dog would come after me and let my brothers and sisters go, but my sister Maggie grabbed me and pulled me back into the buggy. She told me to stay with her and my other three siblings. We used the buggy whip to try and chase the dog away. He acted like he wanted to jump in the buggy, so we were scared. We drove in a driveway hoping someone would help us, but no one came. We turned and continued going on the road until a school bus chased the dog off! Since we were all shaking and scared, we stopped at a house and the people drove us home. We left the horse for Dad to get later.

One other time our horse's hind end went down, and we had to leave him in someone else's barn for a long time. We finally brought him home but had to get rid of him. We now had a horse named Sunny, whom anyone could drive. He was a beautiful dark brown horse with a black mane and tail. Later, you will find out what a tragic and horrible death awaited him.

My fifth-grade teacher was Martha Brenneman from Ashland, Ohio, another Amish community about thirty miles from Fredericktown. It didn't take me long to sense that Teacher Martha didn't like me. She wouldn't hesitate to put me down in front of everybody. Not just me... she did it to others, too. This was just her attitude—very strict and mean. Maybe she was under a lot of

The house my parents purchased in Fredericktown, Ohio.

stress. I don't know, but I did try to stay away from her as far as I could and not cross paths with her too many times.

During our first winter in Fredericktown, a blizzard struck. It was horrible. At the time, we were milking cows, so we had to bundle up really good and hold hands to walk to the barn so we wouldn't get lost on our way out and back. In the meantime, the electric was off, which didn't bother us, but our poor neighbors were freezing. Dad hitched up two work horses and a sled and drove to their house. He returned with the Carvers, an English family with four boys and two girls. They stayed with us in our house for a week. They dressed differently, but otherwise, we were all the same and had fun together. We still did our daily jobs, and they helped us.

Before the next school year started, the community built a new schoolhouse a mile and a half from us on Andy Fisher's property. Now we could walk to school plus the Schlabach's came in this area, too. Finally, William Schlabach and I were at the same schoolhouse and in the same grade at South Darlington School. In the summer, the kids played baseball, peek around the corner, dare base, over the schoolhouse, and cops and robbers. In the winter, we played dodgeball in the basement, ping-pong, and upset the fruit basket. We made our own UNO cards from Blue Bonnet butter boxes, so we played UNO a lot! Grades seven and eight were the same other than a different teacher, Martha Miller.

Mom didn't feel well lots of times, so she spent time at the Carvers' house eating frozen yogurt and making phone calls to take care of the bills and payments for the farm. So, it was like I grew up without a mom. Because she had a weight problem, she walked the road a lot at night. One night she came inside and said a man walked out of the ditch and wanted to walk with her. She was so scared! Another time a neighbor had a huge dog that didn't like Mom walking on their drive, so he bit her leg. Luckily, she didn't bleed too much even though she had lots of varicose veins. She talked about taking it to court but didn't.

Right beside our house was a freeway with all kinds of traffic and big bridges. We used to walk across the bridge and stop to wave at traffic or just watch the cars go by below us. One day we were standing on the bridge above the freeway when one of the cars jammed into the car in front of it because the people were so busy watching us. Believing the accident was our fault, we ran home, and a policeman came and questioned us later. We crossed another bridge every day going to school and back.

Standing on the interstate bridge near our house.

Farming

Every morning, we woke up early to do our chores before school. I milked four cows morning and night. At the most, we had thirty cows. Sometimes, my job was to scrub milk pails and clean the milk house. We always had lots of cats roaming around wanting a drink of milk.

Dad rented a field across the road, so we went there to make hay or husk corn. Since Dad was busy, we children sometimes had to load hay ourselves. Mae, Simon Jr., and I loaded up hay— Simon drove the horses, Mae stomped, and I loaded. Once while I was loading, I meant to stick the fork in the load but stuck it in my bare foot. Ouch! We always went barefooted because there was no money to buy shoes. Our toes had to be really red and

The South Darlington School where I attended sixth through eighth grades.

cold before shoes were allowed. When we fetched the cows in the morning, we would make the cows get up and then we'd stand on the spot where they laid so we could warm our feet.

Dad built a big cement silo for the cows' silage, so we put corn through the shredder when it was ready. I really wanted to go to the top of the silo, but alas, I was too scared! I tried, but the silo was thirty doors high and I barely made it halfway. My sister Maggie had no choice but to crawl to the top every night that we put corn in the silo. I remember her saying the silo seemed higher and higher. She was so scared and was sure Dad would forget that she was up there, but she always made it down alive. Several times, I would go outside to look up to make sure she was okay. Sometimes the Carvers, our English neighbor friends, came over to watch us.

Neighbors

When I was in eighth grade, another family moved in beside us... well, one-and-a-half miles down the road. Daniel Gingerich had a big family, and all his kids were married except three: Everett, Kristie, and Mel. His daughter Charlotte who had five children also lived with him. (Her husband had left her and went English.) Mel was a little older than I and was out of school already. We talked and played together a lot. He played with everyone, but he gave me some extra attention. Then one day, Charlotte's daughter Alice, who was younger than I was, told me Mel liked me, even though he gave my sister Maggie the most attention. William found out about Mel at school one night as we were getting ready to go home. A ball hit me pretty hard in my back. When I looked around, William was busy tying his shoes, but I knew! He didn't like it that I liked someone else. Eli, Alice's brother, was very cute, too. We gave each other attention, but he was quite a bit younger.

One time Mel helped us do our chores while Dad and Mom left to visit. He carved my name in the basement door! I was a little proud. It always felt good to get a boy's attention. Of course, not all the attention was good. He told me he went to my room upstairs and snooped through my autograph book and found a girl named Rosie. In time, Mel drifted away to other girls and married Rosie Byler.

Like I said earlier, I was a tomboy. Ponies were my glory and climbing trees and taking walks were good, too. I was the happiest outside. I loved to make sure other girls and boys were happy and laughing. I wrestled a lot with my brother Simon Jr. who was two years younger than me. I could handle him until he finished school and then he beat me. We tore hair or whatever happened, and we argued about everything. We tried to stay on top of each other to prove that we were better than the other.

— 3 —

Home Life

EIGHTH GRADE IS THE LAST year of Amish school, and we celebrated by having our Eighth Grade Picnic Day and receiving our eighth-grade diploma. That day was fun. Parents brought dinners—potatoes, wieners, salads, cake, pies, ice cream, and drinks. We played round ball. The eighth graders were at bat, and we played until almost noon because no one could get us out! William bragged me up and gave me hints about what direction to bat the ball so I could make a home run. It worked! I batted the ball over the South Darlington Schoolhouse for the first time. I was the first one to ever do it, but later on, more kids did. It was a great feeling!

With school finished, it was home life for me. By now, there were six of us—three boys and three girls. We were always busy. We had an addition added to our barn my first year out which was 1981. They jacked up the barn and put stackers underneath, laid block, and then let the barn back down. It was lots of work, and it was so hot that summer. Even the breeze was hot. Everything was dry and brown. We had a frolic every day with whoever showed up. I remember one day especially because only one guy came, a young man named Leonard Wengard. He was a friend, but nothing special. What made this memory stand out was Leonard was alone. His sisters Rhoda and Sophia were in our group of girls. Leonard will be mentioned again for something special.

Since Dad had no one to help with the chores, I had to help with the after-breakfast chores: clean stalls, make sure horses and cows had hay, sweep the aisle, and put hay in mangers, and put straw down. I never had a fear of horses. I could handle anything—harness, work horses, and all. I was never afraid of cows either. Probably because I was the chore girl. Every night, we took turns throwing silage down. Others weren't afraid to climb, so I rarely did it.

One day I let the horses out, gave them hay, put straw in the stalls, opened the door to let the horses in, and then went to tie them up. Two work horses started to fight, and I just up and slapped one on his butt. He kicked me in the leg. I couldn't believe that he actually kicked me! I was around that horse all the time. He hurt my feelings by kicking me, and I was lame for a while. I realized that he was just a horse, not a friend. After that, I was incredibly careful about walking up behind a horse . . . any horse.

The milk truck came every day. The milk cans were in the trough to pick up. When I was still in school, we milked the cows in a row in the lean-to. They were tied with a chain and snap. Everything was fine until Dad decided to get five or six new cows. When milking time came, these cows had no stall and were scared. They liked nothing better than to start in front of the cows and just bust through all the chains and untie all the cows. Oh, what a mess! Cows everywhere! It took a lot longer to milk on those days. In later years, Dad added another addition to the barn and put stanchions in so we could milk in peace. We all had our own milk chair to sit on, too. We also had a new gutter that was much cleaner and better. Now it was fun to milk cows every morning and every night.

When plowing needed to be done, I plowed with my team of horses, George and Joe, and a walking plow. I usually lost a lot of pounds walking and plowing. Dad took the big double plow and three or four horses. Later on, I had the chance to plow with a single riding plow and three horses. That was fun!

I don't remember much about housework because my sister Maggie did that. However, with a large Amish family, we always had big laundries to do. We had to heat our water in a big kettle and use a pail to dump the hot water into the machine to wash clothes. We hung the clean clothes outside, winter and summer. Winter laundry froze on the line and was double the work. Oh, those were days to remember! One time I was sent with Maggie to start a fire underneath the kettle to heat water to wash. I accidentally put gas in a jug instead of kerosene, and the hair on Maggie's arms, her eyebrows, and her eyelashes burned off! Maggie's eyebrows and lashes have been darker ever since. I felt so bad and sorry.

When I was fifteen, I had a sore tooth and went to the dentist to have it pulled. I got dry socket in it and had to take strong pain pills. Early in the morning around four or five o'clock, I woke up in a lot of pain. I took four strong pills and didn't wake up until evening chore time. I didn't realize the pills would knock me out! All I wanted was away from the pain. Lesson learned.

My brothers kept their coon dogs locked in a building and did they ever stink! I stayed away from them. One night we heard a racket, so some of us went to check out the noise. We followed the sound and discovered that my brother Brian had a coon in the empty silo along with a coon hound. He was training his dog. Brian was a coon hunter, and I went coon hunting with him once but didn't like it.

One evening around dusk, my older sister Maggie and younger sister Mae were resting with me by the swings Dad had made in the front yard. A cornfield with thick, high corn was not far from the swings. We faced the field and had our backs toward the yard and house. Suddenly, we saw a white object, about eight rows in, move forward ten feet then turn around and go back ten feet. We were so scared that we couldn't move. No one said anything, and then I said, "Let's go inside the house." We stood and started walking with our backs to the white object. Suddenly something grabbed my arm and yelled. I dropped to the ground crying! I was so scared! It was Simon Jr. with a big white farm cat that he'd been holding and moving back and forth in the cornfield. Moments like that were so scary and frightening. They've never left me. I am in my late forties today and still feel the same feeling that I felt back then.

Another time my mother asked me to go downstairs at night to get something, so I did. Our stairways were open in the middle. When I was going back upstairs, I saw white eyes and white teeth looking at me from under the stairs. I ran up and started crying.

My dad came upstairs laughing. He had scared me! Another night I was sent out to get kerosene after dark. When I reached the barn to fill the jug, someone popped out from behind the barrel and screamed at me. I screamed even louder, fell to the ground, and just laid there. My sister Maggie felt bad because she didn't think it would scare me so much. My life was already so messed up! Or so it seemed to me. More work followed and time went on.

Accidents

We had so many accidents in our family, over and over. When I was about fifteen, we bailed hay all day and loaded it in the hayloft. We had a bridge built across the aisle of the hayloft, and as we finished filling the loft full, we walked underneath it. As we walked "through," it busted down. We all escaped except Maggie. We were frightened so badly that it wasn't funny. We started throwing bales away, away, away until we finally found Maggie. She was alive, but her back was very sore. She was a lucky girl!

One Sunday we were driving to church at our neighbor Daniel's house and Mom didn't go. We were going downhill at a fairly good pace when Peggy, our horse, dodged a dump truck, jumped on top of a mailbox, and rammed the post up into her stomach. We turned, went back home, and had to put Peggy down because she would have never survived.

On another day, we were thrashing oats all day long working as hard as we could. It was a very busy day with a wonderful crop. Thrashing oats is done by hitching two or four horses to an Amish combine to cut the oats and separate the straw from the grain. Oats go into a wagon and the straw blows into a hay baler. The bales of straw go up the elevator into the haymow and get stacked for winter when it's used to keep animals dry and warm. At the end of the day, Dad left the machine outside the barn and fixed the blower into the straw bin. We cleaned up, ate supper, took our baths, and went to bed. Early the next morning, someone woke us up yelling, "Fire! Fire! Fire!" We all went running outside and raked straw away from the barn as fast and hard as we could. The fire came to the barn and stopped. It burned the wood of the blower off. We never knew what stopped that fire; only God knows.

That same day, we ate supper, and after chores, we all gathered around the house. It was foggy and almost dark when we realized that my brother Simon Jr. was missing. We started a search party and hunted everywhere. Suddenly, I kicked against something hard, and I knew that it was Simon and that he was dead. I started crying loudly and yelled that I had found him, but I believed it was too late. One of the others came around with a flashlight. The light shone on the shoes that I had kicked. We pulled him out and discovered that he had crawled under the bales and fell asleep. He was fine! I was so scared, but happy he was okay.

Hired Work

A man came out to our Amish community one day looking for girls to help pick berries for his store at Henderson Strawberry Farm. I went with him around the community, and we gathered up a load of twelve or thirteen girls. We picked the strawberries and placed them in four-quart baskets. Those days were long and busy. Because I was the boss of the crew, I wrote out checks for everyone. Henderson would take me to McDonald's on paydays. It took all day. Another guy named Gilbert had a strawberry patch and another load of girls picked for him. Anna Yoder was the boss of that load.

In the summer, we pulled weeds and picked strawflowers for Henderson's wife, Merilee. She sold lots of baby's breath. Henderson had two big ponds to use for irrigating his berries, so on days that we didn't pick berries, we drove to his farm to fish. He had beautiful, big bluegills in there ... lots of them. He also had catfish. I caught a catfish one day and was so scared that I threw my pole. A friend grabbed the pole and pulled him out. The fish was twenty-nine inches long and weighed six pounds. I took the fish home to show my family and then took him back to the pond and threw him in.

Because I was a tomboy, I was the hired hand on our farm to do "run around" work. I drove about six miles one way to our neighbor James Raber's house to get bulk food, such as flour, sugar, yeast, and baking powder. I had to drive past the Schlabach's farm on the way, so I always kept my eyes open for William. Now that we were out of school, I didn't see him anymore because he was in another church district. I spotted him once when he was plowing in the field, but he was too far off to talk to. We just waved. I have no idea if he knew that it was me, but I knew it was him! William's family also had a strawberry patch, so we picked there a couple of times, too. By then, William and I were too shy to talk. We would pick not too far apart, but not too close either.

Sometimes we received loads and loads of outdated baked goods, such as raspberry and vanilla Danish rolls, lots of Twinkies, pies, bread, maple rolls, and donuts. Our big surrey would be piled full with outdated food. I drove the surrey around to the Amish farmers and sold the baked goods for half price. This took me all day, and I would be so tired by nighttime after driving all around and crawling up and down, in and out of the buggy.

Visitors

Both of my parent's families were from Geauga County. Mom's side was from Farmington, Dad's side was from the Mespo area, and Uncle Boyd was from Parkman, Ohio. We occasionally went to visit them for weddings and funerals. I remember my younger aunts' weddings since they were closer to my age. Noah Byler married Aunt Ruby. Ervin married Anna, and my sister Maggie was a table waiter at their wedding. Aunt Edith married David Gingerich and had several children. Then she left the Amish, although I don't know why. Today she is happily married to another man, and her life has changed dramatically.

Every now and then, family visited. Their visits were rare though. I remember the time all dad's family (his parents, Edwin and Naomi, and his siblings—Lily, Lucille, James, Larry, Harry, Wanda, and Nora) came for a visit. We enjoyed the day with them, and in the afternoon while we were in the living room, I smelled smoke! I asked Mom about it because I thought the stove was puffing. She smiled and said, "No, Uncle Edward was smoking a cigarette." I was so embarrassed, and he was, too. After that, the uncles all went outside to smoke.

Later, Mom's side of the family came: her parents, David and Edith Miller, and her brother and sisters and several cousins—David Jr., Kathleen, Barbara, Sarah, Eleanor, Audrey, and Rose. Some were married, too, with their families. When we heard they were coming we cleaned the house like spring cleaning inside and out. My mom's side was from higher-up church people; they were cleaner and more modern than Dad's side. We were tuckered out by the time they arrived.

Part 2
The Meeting

— 4 —

Sixteen

I'M NOW SIXTEEN YEARS OLD. Mom didn't have time to sew a coat for me, so I went to Widow Selena Miller. She sewed for other people, and she made the coat for me. I requested that she make it form-fitting. It was my first time having the nerve to ask someone to make my clothes "fit"—against Amish rules! I was always a neat, clean, and proper attitude person with my clothes not too tight, but not too loose, either. It felt good to have something that fit me exactly right.

That year, Dad added a wash house to our house. No more basement washing. We moved our cupboards out there for storage. I remember doing a lot of cleaning, and I removed electric wires from all around. We had a dirt basement in front, and I also cleaned that. Then Dad added a new pantry in our kitchen, so we re-did the kitchen, too. It was a mess but nice when it was done. Our kitchen was always long and lean with a huge table on the side of the wall.

The first or second year after I was out of school, we had a sugar house. I carried buckets of sap to the wagon until I got a stiff neck that was so bad I had to go to the doctor. The pain was almost unbearable.

Tragedy

After a long day of doing hay, a letter came in the mail saying the Mullets, my dad's side of the family, were coming to visit. We were excited! They said they had hay to put in their barn before they came to our house, but they never made it. The next day we received word that Uncle Harry had been struck by lightning and killed. Now, instead of them coming to visit, we were going to Geauga County for a funeral. I was so sad. Harry and I were always close.

Before we left for the funeral, we worked to finish our hay. I was looking out over the fields when I saw something white waving in the air. I said something to Dad, but neither of us could figure out what it was. The next morning, a big white goose was in our front yard and came close enough to the house to look in the window. Dad went outside, and somehow, he got the goose to walk to the barn. He put a cage over the goose and came back inside to eat breakfast. When we were done eating, we children all went out to look at the goose, it was gone! There was no way it crawled out underneath the cage, and the cage door was closed. We will never know how it escaped.

Uncle Harry's funeral was sad. I cried my heart out. I missed

The Meeting

The cemetery where Uncle Henry and a lot of my relatives are buried.

him so much. When the gravediggers carried the coffin into the house, I thought I would cry my insides out. It was very hard seeing my uncle and friend being carried away forever.

More Farm Work

That same summer, we were making hay again, and everyone was helping that possibly could. Dad had a habit of having horses that weren't safe, and on this day, we had a team that wasn't the safest. Mae's job was driving the team, and before she climbed up onto the wagon, the team took off. Mae was too stubborn to drop the reins, so she was dragged between the horses and the wagon on her stomach. When she finally stopped the horses, a bolt on the wagon poked too far into her hip. She was a sick girl for quite a time, but she was one lucky girl because the outcome could have been worse. I frequently checked on her in the house to make sure she was okay or to see if she needed something.

I will never forget the rows and rows of corn we husked by hand. Sometimes the day was cold, and sometimes it was a hot autumn day. Husking corn was done by four or five people walking down the rows of corn picking and husking the corn and throwing it on the wagon drawn by two horses. We always called out to the horses—"Kiddap" to go and "Whoa" to stop. Sometimes we had runaways, but not too often. When the wagon was full, we drove up to the corncrib and threw the corn on the motorized elevator that loaded the corn into the crib for winter use.

We ground our own feed for the animals with a grinder also run by a huge motor. Dad mixed corn, oats, and minerals on a pile in layers. One person scooped the corn mixture and another person bagged it and stacked it against the wall. We also made our own chicken feed.

The community needed a new place for a schoolhouse, so Dad let them use our pasture. The schoolhouse was just a simple, one-room building. Sadie Wengard was the first teacher, and sometimes I would substitute for her. I liked being the substitute even though a little Swartz boy and a Raber boy gave me a really hard time and then just laughed at me. Later, Ava Mae was the teacher. She slept at our house except on the weekends. The next year Nila Byler taught. She also slept at our house, and we were good friends. My brother Jonathan was her student and later ended up marrying her.

My brother Brian was playing in school when suddenly we

all heard crying. At high speed, we ran back and looked to see why he was crying. He had a wire stuck through his foot! It went in the bottom and came out by his ankle. I looked at it and left for the garden as fast as I could to pull weeds. I pass out if I see blood from someone else. Dad told Brian "Grit your teeth" and took a pair of pliers and pulled out the wire. Someone put peroxide on his foot and ankle and bandaged it.

— 5 —

Seventeen

My sister Maggie found a boyfriend, Victor Mast, in Ashland, Ohio. When his sister got married, Maggie went to the wedding. After the wedding, I went with a driver for thirty miles to bring her back. Victor had a brother whom I was introduced to that night, but nothing came of it.

I met a girl Ruth Shrock from Ashland, and we started writing. Maggie was friends with Ruth's sister Sara and had visited Sara one time while in Ashland. Now friends from Ashland started to mix in and out with the Mullet girls. Salina Troyer was another friend plus many others.

More Home Life

Winters were normal; summers were usual. One of my jobs at home was getting up every morning to pack lunches. Another job was helping Mom with the chickens she butchered for others for extra income. I stayed up late at night to help clean the meat and make sure all the feathers were off. Sometimes Mae took turns with me.

That September, my sister Abigail was born. Maggie was the maid, and again I did the "run around" jobs. I started having headaches, and my eyes hurt. I had my eyes checked, but the doctor said that I didn't need glasses.

We babysat a new family's children quite a few times. They were the Joshua Raber family with children—Albert, Elsie, Velma, Maynard, John, Dean, and Millie. Sometimes we helped with the Raber's crops as well. We watched their kids grow up like our own family.

One of the first things we did after I turned seventeen was sell all our cows. Dad couldn't make enough money anymore, so we had a sale on the home farm. It was hard seeing all our cows spread out all over the world. How I missed our cows. I often wondered if they were okay and if they were being treated right. So, now, in 1984, my family turned from farmers to carpenters.

Another Accident

After I turned seventeen, I started my first job as a maid working for others. What a different life I had now. No more plowing, husking, or chores.

Dennis and Lorna Gingerich needed a maid, so I went. I washed for them twice a week and helped out during the day.

Every night, I went home. One day while traveling to the Gingerich's, I came to the intersection at State Route 546. Pine tree limbs hung out too far making it difficult to see the traffic on 546. Thinking it was clear, I told my horse Sunny to go. Halfway across the highway, I heard a loud horn. I can still hear that horn to this day! I slapped Sunny with the reins and thought I was safe. CRASH!!! I felt and saw a minivan cross the road ahead of me. That's the last I remember.

When all was done, my buggy laid tipped over in a field. I crawled out with a sore shoulder. I looked around for Sunny. I walked up the road and there my horse lay in the middle of the road with his head off. His bridle was about 100 yards down the road with his head in it. I was in shock. There went my beautiful Sunny horse.

Soon blinking lights showed up, and the police arrived. Someone asked me to sit in the back of the police car to answer questions. A guy in the front seat told me he was the driver of the minivan. He said he was sorry, he could have gone behind me, but he didn't want to hit the buggy for my safety.

After the accident, my mind froze up for many days before it healed again. Nobody talked to me about the accident. I got over it myself. I was a lucky girl!

Another memory that stands out to me from when I was a maid was the time I took the place of Bonnie Fisher. She was the maid for the Glicks who had just welcomed little Mattie into their family. Bonnie had to attend a wedding, so I took her place. I remember making applesauce in a little kettle. It was so different making just enough for one meal. I had to sleep in the basement that night. What a scary experience! I wasn't used to being alone, let alone at a friend's place. I was glad when morning came.

Learning Rules

Vincent Hershberger, Stella Fisher, and I took instruction class for baptism during the summer of 1984. I was baptized that August by Daniel Gingerich, our bishop at the time. In instruction class, we found out the rules and regulations we needed to follow. Lots of rules. Rules for everything. Very strict, too.

Rules for appearance included what clothes we could wear, how we sewed them, and how we wore them. They could not be tight or form-fitting, and they needed one-and-a-half-inch seams, one-inch size for the collar, and the belt with one-and-a-quarter-inch seams. Baby blankets couldn't be fringy and bright. And there was even a rule about certain types of windows in our houses.

Haircuts were allowed but just a circle around the head. The difference between a man and a boy happens once he started instruction class. The boys had to leave a hairline for a beard. They could cut the length off until they were married. After marriage, they could not trim it anymore. (The rule about beard trimming will be significant later on in my life.) A girl must comb her hair a certain way, not back up over her head. We also were not allowed to show too much hair under our covering.

Traditionally, the girls in the instruction class planned what color dress to wear from one church Sunday to the next. But, of course, Sunday dress had rules. Every other time, we wore black. Black and navy blue were the main Amish colors women wore to church among my group. We could wear green, teal, brown, or gray, but it had to be darker shades, nothing bright and flashy. We wore black shoes and socks plus a black cap. Once a girl married, she wore a white cap fixed exactly like the black cap.

Even the horses and buggies had rules. Buggies had to have "slow moving" triangle signs, blinkers, and lanterns in a box for lights. Cushion seats were dark colors, but no green. Robes and blankets had to be plain and dark-colored. Tape had to be a certain length, and no short trimmings. Horses had to be plain colors with not too much white and no paint horses. Harnesses had to be plain, not too many white or silver rings for flashy, braided lines to drive. No rein check—the horse wasn't allowed to hold its head too high. Nothing fancy!

We were not allowed to have a phone in our house, but we could use an English neighbor's phone or write letters. Electricity was also forbidden. We were permitted to ride in a car, but not allowed to drive it. We had to pay a driver to take us wherever we needed to go if we were not taking the horse and buggy. No hot water system in the house, but we were allowed to have supply tanks for water. Toilets were permitted but most did not have one.

Carpenters and farmers had rules, too. Carpenters could use electric tools but could not own them. Machinery had to have all steel wheels, no soft tires. No tires on buggy wheels either, only steel wheels. Milk was to be stored in milk cans only, no bulk milk tanks allowed. A huge uproar had gone through our community when we were still milking cows. Some people wanted the bulk tanks; some didn't. The huge ruckus finally ended with the rule about no milking machines and no bulk tanks.

– 6 –

Decisions

Turning seventeen meant I was now part of the youngie group. I had my mind on the youngie a lot. I attended singings every Sunday. The first Sunday was so scary, and I felt lost. Yes, William was there and saw me, but he was going steady with Sara Wengard. He looked so grown and different.

Like I mentioned earlier, I attended lots of weddings. I usually ended up with nobody, someone nobody else wanted, or a total stranger at the weddings. That year, Willard Hershberger and Lillian Shrock were married. Lots of my youngie friends from Ashland attended the wedding. I spotted a handsome guy with long black hair and blue eyes. His looks caught my attention. I found out that he was Martin Shrock's son Elias. Imagine my excitement when I was asked to pair up with him to sit at the table the night of the wedding. I was overjoyed! We talked very little, but we enjoyed each other's presence. When Ruth Shrock, the girl I was writing to, walked by the door, I asked Elias if she was his sister. He said "yes," and I was surprised. This boy was Ruth's brother! While we were eating supper, William somehow had an eye on me; I could feel it and caught him watching me. "Oh well," I thought, "Whatever!"

From our school days, William's sister Madeline and I were good friends. One night, she asked if I had a ride to the singing from James Raber's to Albert Miller's. When I told her no, she said I could go with her and William. I was excited! We all had an enjoyable time.

The next Sunday, I sat beside Sara Wengard and thought that maybe William would stop, and sure enough, he did. My sister Maggie's boyfriend, Victor, had come for the weekend, so I invited the Frank Schlabach and David Byler youngie to our house to play volleyball in the afternoon. It rained... no luck. So, we ganged up to go to the singing at James Raber's. I went with Elijah and Neva Byler, and Mae went with William and Madeline. Later I found out that William was disappointed. I was too, but because Neva and I were best friends, I knew I should go with her.

Shortly after that, I received a letter from Elias Shrock saying that he wanted to start writing. I was confused. Yes, I wanted to write to Elias, but I had William in mind. I didn't know what to do, so I refused Elias. Then William asked me for a date after the singing. Later, I found out that he said never again. But Neva said if he says never again, he usually does ask again. And he did! Somehow, I ended up in Ashland between dates with William when Elias asked me on a date. So, I had my first date with Elias.

Now I was really confused. I liked both William and Elias.

I almost lost my mind. My mom said she never knew two boys could mess up a girl's mind like these two did to me. I didn't eat or sleep hardly at all. Finally, my dad said, "Make up your mind! One or the other is not for you." A daughter always likes to please her dad with a boyfriend . . . or I did. I could just tell that Dad liked William but disliked Elias. One morning as I was packing lunch, I had to walk across to the neighbors to get lunch meat. As I walked out of the house, it was still dark. I spotted a man in white standing in the driveway. I instinctively knew that it was Jesus! When I came close to Him, He said, "If you marry Elias, you will get to heaven." A promise! I went through tears and pain giving up my first love, but I turned my back on William. I wrote to Elias and said, "I changed my mind. I'll go with you after all." This choice ripped my heart out and tore it to pieces.

Dating Years

My dates with Elias were parted to every three weeks. Elias drove thirty miles to our house with his horse and buggy for the first three-week period. Then three weeks later, I went up to Ashland with a driver. I usually took Tom Henderson as my driver. We did this steadily for almost three years. It was not fun to go to singings anymore, watching all the steadies every Sunday night while I was by myself. I was so sad, and I cried often. Elias wasn't allowed to attend every wedding because his church didn't allow him to attend too often. Why not? It was a *wedding*! So, weddings weren't fun for me anymore either.

The Meeting

One of the wooded paths Elias and I walked frequently while dating.

Don't get me wrong—Elias and I had fun times, too, but I was forced to go along with rules that weren't mine. The Ashland community's rules were very strict. They allowed only rocking chairs or love seats for dates. In my mind, that was ridiculous. I'd never heard of such rules, but Elias would be punished if we didn't follow the rules, so we did. I had never used a rocking chair, but we had a love seat.

Elias was different. He was way too polite compared to what I grew up with. I grew up with the truth. We didn't bend words to make them look or sound nice. We used them exactly for what they were. For example, if a child had a diaper filled, we said the baby pooped himself or he or she is all fa pooped. Elias told me that I couldn't say that anymore. He said I had to say that the baby had a messy diaper. It was too harsh to say "poop." While that might seem insignificant, I could feel myself being torn away from my family one step at a time. I no longer used "harsh" words. I stepped further and further away from "the truth" in words, which also took me away from the truth in other ways. Elias also told me on our second or third date that I seemed like an "English" girl to him. I was amazed that he felt that way. I had lots of thoughts about English people and liked them and their lifestyle. Elias picked up on my interest, and I don't think he liked it.

When William found out that I had picked Elias as my boyfriend, he said to me, "Elias is going to put you under the buggy seat and forget about you." Years later I remembered those words and wondered, "How did William know?"

One of the first times I was in Ashland singing, I went out to Elias's buggy, climbed on, and just as we started, he drove into a post by the driveway and tipped the buggy over. No one was hurt, but we were dirty, muddy, and shaken up. I blamed him for doing it on purpose. It seemed like he sensed that I loved someone else.

We courted for three years with lots of weekends and visits. The Fredericktown youngie drove up to Ashland on the weekends, and I would accompany them so I could see Elias. Lots of times, he made the thirty-mile drive to my house alone in a horse and buggy. For our dates, we shared the house with Elias's sister Sara and her boyfriend Joseph at the Shrock's and with Ray Jr. and my sister Mae at the Mullets. We took turns either in the kitchen or the living room.

Sadie Miller was a friend of mine who also had a boyfriend from another community. Then she was published to be married to Lester Hershberger. They invited all the youngie to their wedding except the ones from other settlements. She was allowed to invite the others, and since she had a boyfriend from another community, she knew how hard it was to skip weekends with a boyfriend. I didn't believe it when I heard the others weren't invited, so I drove all way to her house one night to ask her why, but she wasn't there. Her sister-in-law told me that it was true. I cried. I chose to not attend Sadie's wedding.

Later, she asked me why I didn't come. She said, "I put the ones who didn't have their boys there in the corner right beside us so they could be with the others in the living room."

I asked her, "What do I want in your corner?" and walked away. To this day, I don't understand why Sadie decided to not invite the others.

Elias and I had our first experience as "side sitters" at his sister Sara's wedding to Joseph Wengard. Sara's wedding was my first time in a bridal party. Since I was at a different settlement, I didn't know lots of people there, but I made new friends. The whole wedding was different because the Ashland community didn't have evening weddings. Their young folks go to the table in the afternoon. Evenings are just for the immediate family, the aunts and uncles from the girl's side only.

Not long after Sara's wedding, my sister Maggie and Victor Mast were married. Elias and I were side sitters for their wedding too. This time I was more relaxed. Because I was used to my people and the way we did things, it was more fun than Sara's wedding.

While dating Elias, I met a lot of new people. One weekend Elias and I plus Elias's sister Rachel and her boyfriend Alan drove to the small Amish community of Jeromesville. We spent the weekend, but I mostly remember that it was a cold trip. After another weekend date, Elias and quite a few other youngie, his cousins, traveled to Michigan by train. He stayed a couple of weeks at his Aunt Laura's house to help out. I met his aunt, uncles, and cousins from all over. He came from big families—a huge group of Shrocks and a huge group of Millers on his mother's side.

Wedding Day — May 18, 1989

Elias and I had planned to marry in November 1988, but my sister Abigail was born that year, so we had to wait. Before we married, I told Elias about my life, how hard it was for me to choose whom to marry, and what had happened. I wanted him to know everything before he said his marriage vows.

Our wedding day . . . finally!! We were published at Michael Glick's church and had our wedding date set for Thursday, May 11, 1989, but alas, William, who was going with Jessie Byler, was published the same day without telling us and also had their date set for May 11. We had some discussion between the four of us, and Elias and I ended up changing our date to May 18. Having to change our date because William was getting married was very hard for me. But May 11 was a cold, rainy day, so we didn't miss anything. I was a table waiter for William and Jessie's wedding, but my mind was on our day.

Lots of work had to be done to get ready for the "Big Day."

The Meeting

Dad decided to add a wrap-around porch to our house before the wedding. I didn't feel like working much because my mind was full of other things. I was inviting people, buying presents and candy, plus helping get dishes from neighbors and getting ready for a serious step in my life. I had lots on my mind. In fact, life seemed like a tornado to me. Elias was still different than me. So different. We disagreed on presents for the cooks and table waiters and how to wrap them. How would our married life turn out?

On the Sunday between William's wedding and my wedding, Elias and I went to Ashland to spend the weekend with the Shrocks and invite friends face to face. We came back home on that Monday. People started coming to help us get ready as our time came closer and closer. One night before our wedding day, I ended up in tears from too much stress, but I did feel better afterward.

Our wedding day was a beautiful day. Perfect. After the morning church services, we were married by Edwin, my grandfather on my dad's side. Our wedding took place in our barn hayloft. Because we didn't have a hill to the loft, Dad had built a stairway up into the barn. We had around three hundred people in attendance. Our side sitters were my sister Mae and Ray Miller, Elias's sister Rachel and Alan Miller. Eck cooks (the ones who prepared the meal for the corner table where Elias and I sat) were our sisters Maggie and Sara. My brother Simon Jr. and Elias's brother Silas were hostlers, the ones who took care of all the horses.

In the afternoon we opened presents. We received lots of nice things. Our friends did well! Then we watched others play ball, and in the evening, we had a living room full of young folks. After the singing finished, our wedding was over. Our first night sleeping together was an experience no words can express. We were both bashful. However, it was nice that Elias didn't have to leave to go home anymore.

The next day, we cleared away the mess, and everyone left. We had no place to live yet, so I put my things in boxes and used my room upstairs as our house. I helped Mom, and Elias helped Dad with his carpentry.

— 7 —

Disagreement

EXACTLY ONE WEEK AFTER OUR married life began, Elias and Dad got into a huge argument about Joshua in the Bible. Did Joshua call for the sun to stand still or the earth to stand still? They argued for about thirty minutes.

The next morning after breakfast while everyone, including big and little brothers and sisters, was in the kitchen, Dad started yelling at Elias in front of the whole family.

Dad ordered Elias—"Never do you ever say such things about one of the Bible men ever again. If you do, you will never speak to any of the other kids in my family ever again!"

I was one of Dad's kids. Just married. Can you imagine how I felt? Horrible, wicked, scared. I cried until my eyes were bright red. Their argument put some awful bad feelings and hurts in hearts. Hard to forgive. My dad and Elias didn't get along well at all, nor did Elias get along with his own dad which often made me sad.

New Home

A couple of weeks later, we found out that Ed Miller, our old neighbor, was electrocuted and killed. He used to be a minister in our church but had moved further away. His was the first funeral Elias and I attended after we were married. Ed is a friend and neighbor never forgotten.

Uncle Emmett Shrock paid a visit and said that he knew an English guy, Bob Westbrook, who wanted someone to do chores for him. So, Elias started a new job. Bob paid good money, but he lived nine miles away. After a few weeks, Bob said he had a house we could live in so Elias could do the job and not have to travel every day. It was so far away from my family and out of our church district, but we went. Bob's wife Mary was short-tempered, as we had heard, and it wasn't long until she and Elias got into a fight about a newborn calf.

Our house was older, and it was huge. When winter came, the house was cold! I kept a coat on 24/7. I spent time cleaning the house since it was a mess with things the previous residents had left behind. The garage was especially messy. After a while, I became bored, so I spent time up at the farm with Elias and Bob. Then someone started me on quilting. I quilted for $.30 a yard. I began with wall hangings. The first one I ever made was so bad that the lady said she couldn't pay me, but the second one was better. Now I had extra work to do.

Every week on Wednesdays, I drove nine miles to go home to my folks as "gather day." It was a long drive alone there and back. Lady, our horse, was mean about running out of the shafts. You'd

The Meeting

better make sure you had all the snaps loose. But she was a good traveler on the road. Then my sister Mae and her boyfriend Ray planned to marry and wanted me there to help. My family complained that by the time I showed up the day was half gone plus I had to leave early because it was a long distance to home. So, I started off at five o'clock in the morning. It was scary driving all by myself through the dark, but it made my day at home longer. I hated those lonely rides!

Mom gave me a sewing machine and said that it was mine if I helped her sew shirts for my brothers and dresses for my sisters. I sewed clothes in between quilting. Those were long days I'll never forget. My first washing machine was round, and my first wash line was twine tied from one tree to the next.

Across from our driveway was a little pond. Sometimes, after chores, we fished in the pond. I learned all about fishing plus how to fry them. In the evenings, we played games—Rook and UNO—a lot.

This was pretty much our life while Elias worked for Bob. We didn't meet many others since we lived two miles outside of the outskirts of Amish country. My mom and my sisters and children visited me twice while I lived in the big old house. They talked about how far away I was. I knew the journey was tiresome, especially alone! The Shrocks came by once for supper and spent the evening.

During our time in the old house, I took my first trip as a wife to the bulk food store. Elias thought I spent too much money! I spent around eighty dollars.

Also, for the first time in my life, I went to Mount Hope

Machinery Sale. What a different experience. I was new at the sale and new to walking at the sale with my new husband.

Moving Back Home

Bob decided to sell his cows so that meant we were out of a job and house. My dad said we could build a trailer-type house on his property behind the big house. We bought lumber, and in July 1990 we moved into our new house. No more long rides for me. We were also back in our church again.

Even though we paid for our little house we put in the back yard, we used a small corner in Dad's basement for our canning goods. I used the wash house, too. Our buggy was stored outside, but the horse used one stall in the barn. My parents decided that we should pay rent. Since my sister Mae was married now, my mom needed help. Our rent consisted of me working for Mom three days a week, Elias mowing the backyard, and us paying fifty dollars per month. For my part, the rent wouldn't have been so bad if it wasn't for the wall between my husband and my dad. The feeling I experienced was awful. They never talked to each other and had a very bad connection. If Dad did say something to Elias, it was a mean remark of some kind.

Not long after we moved back, the three-day measles popped out. I was pregnant at the time, which meant the measles were dangerous for me. I stayed in our house. Elias went to church, but luckily, he didn't get the measles or bring them home to me.

On my days at home, I quilted and advanced from wall hangings to big quilts. Working three days a week for my mom didn't leave many days left for me. Even on days when Elias wasn't at work, I still had to go and help Mom.

When we moved back, Elias joined my dad's carpentry crew which consisted of my brothers and my brother-in-law Ray. Elias would come home from work feeding my mind with things like "Dad likes Ray better than me." If Ray didn't do something right, my dad would explain to him how to do it, but if Elias did something wrong, Dad would yell at him and say bad things like "You're just acting stupid" or "You should do better." This unfair treatment didn't help matters any or help our bad feelings. Elias was now between me and my family, separating us.

We could be with my family anytime we wanted, so we just hid our feelings. Lots of times I felt depressed. Before I met Elias, I was always on good terms with my family. But because my brothers didn't really like Elias either, it made things worse for me. I was close to my brothers, but now we drifted apart. I could sense that Elias's family didn't like us or me the best either. They wouldn't say so, but I sensed it. I now lived in a world one step away from both families. I didn't agree with Elias's way of life either, but I was married, so I was stuck in a very miserable world and all alone. So many days I cried my heart out and spoke to the One who would always have His ways of comforting me. I could feel God's presence very near.

A couple of months after our wedding, I started having miscarriages. I finally went to the doctor who diagnosed me with ovarian cysts. The doctor scheduled me for an operation, which went well. Soon after, I kept my pregnancy and started working for Tom Henderson's Strawberry Patch again.

The usual summer and winter days passed by. In July 1991, our first baby, a son, was born. Dale weighed eight pounds two ounces. He was a good baby. Having a little boy changed our life into a different world.

Tragedies

Dale was only a couple of weeks old when a tragic accident happened in the Fredericktown community. Sarah Miller, her daughter Clara, her son Noah, her married daughter Esther and her husband Aden Yoder, along with their five children, went to visit another of Sarah's daughters for an evening of fun and supper. On their way home, a drunken driver with a suspended driver's license hit their buggy from behind, killing the horse, shattering the buggy, and scattering the family's bodies all over the field, ditch, and road. Everyone except four of Aden and Esther's children died that night. Esther was pregnant at the time and the baby was also killed. Six caskets at the same funeral. I could only go one evening. An incredibly sad and tragic event for everyone.

At the same time, my brother Harry had a brain tumor and was like a vegetable until he was eight years old. It took lots of special care and doctor treatments, everywhere. One day I had to take Harry to the doctor because Dad and Mom were busy. He was getting his treatments in Holmes County. The lady driver who took me was friendly, and she taught me a song. She told me

The Meeting

I needed the song in my life. At the time, I thought it was strange because I didn't even know her personally. We sang the song all the way up there and back home so I could learn it and sing it alone. The song was "Blessed Assurance"—"This is my story, this is my song, praising my Savior all the day long!" Elvin Edith and her daughter were with me. A day to remember.

Samuel Wickey was also involved in Harry's sickness. Samuel treated people with herbs and vitamins, and he pulled sicknesses from people with his hands. He dissolved Harry's tumor, but it left him like a vegetable. Samuel and Dad talked a lot about church problems, and they both got in trouble. At one point, Samuel was shunned. I still don't understand all of what happened. I believe too much talking was involved, and it got my dad in trouble, too. Dad had a bad habit of asking shunned people for advice. Not a wise choice.

Harry died in 1991 on Thanksgiving Day from pneumonia. He was buried in the cemetery by the north corner of the Darlington Church. Mom cried so much. Dale was only a tiny baby and came down with a bad earache. Talk about crying! We put onions on his ear and used eardrops. Lots of church people helped us during this time of grief.

Moving Again

We lived behind my parents' house until we bought a ten-acre field from our neighbors, Earl and Carol Carver. Carol would become a very good friend of our children. Earl was a drunkard but never bothered any of us. Moving to our ten acres put us, again, in a different church district.

We built a nice big house, a little barn, which later became our shop, and a bigger barn. Our upstairs had just walls with no insulation or drywall. Elias painted the barn whenever time permitted and also put siding on our house. Someone gave us a small building for chickens, so we had our own eggs plus we had a goat for milk and one horse. We shopped for our groceries at the gas station in Johnsville. The bulk food store was at Albert Wengard's where they also had a harness shop. I often walked to the country store at Lester Troyer's while my boys slept at the noon hour.

When we built our house, we installed a crank-out window above our sink so I could reach to open the window when I was pregnant. One day, the ministers from the North Church, our new church district, knocked on our door and said, "No crank-out windows allowed!" We were ordered to change the window before the next communion service, which we did. My dad found out about what happened and said that the only reason we had to change the window was because I was one of his kids and Bishop Charles Kauffman didn't like my dad. I didn't think that was true at all.

Elias worked hard for many hours putting a fence around our field for pasture. Our neighbors were the Emory Millers across the field, the Lester Troyers across the field and over the road, and the John Schlabachs down the street from us. Their work horses had a habit of visiting us during the night and eating our garden and my flowers, which made the fence a necessity.

After we moved, Elias changed jobs because Dad didn't have

The first house and barns that Elias and I built together.

enough work for Elias and Ray both. Elias worked for his cousin Wayne Shrock before joining our neighbor Ned Byler's crew. Elias and Ned got along well, and Ned soon had Elias working as the second boss whenever Ned couldn't be there. Well, that was until my dad stuck his nose between Ned and Elias and caused more friction. I nearly hated my dad for always ruining good things and destroying the peace in our lives. Even with my dad's meddling, Ned and Elias remained friends and helped each other out when needed.

My life continued with housework, washing clothes, ironing, cleaning, baking, and cooking. I made all my clothes, and Susannah Troyer taught me how to make coats.

Later on, the Shrocks came to visit for a weekend. They drove down from Ashland with double horses and a big surrey. They had one horse who was very mean, and we had a scary ride home when we went fishing that Saturday at our neighbor's pond. We stopped at a gas station and for ice cream for supper. The Mullets visited now and then.

When our son Mark was born in March 1993, our neighbor lady had a baby the same day with the same midwife. Some exciting moments! Mark has a "twin" although they don't know each other and never met. Mark was a good baby, too, but a bottle was better for him. He liked baby cereal cold in his bottle. He grew very chubby, but later no one would know.

When our next son Eddie was born in August 1994, we bought a regular-size bunk bed and cut it down to a six-year-old crib size for Dale and Mark to sleep in. My parents and their children visited after Eddie was born. They brought their Pomeranian puppy and asked Dale if he would trade a puppy for Baby Eddie. Dale emphatically said, "NO!" Many years later, my dad would take Eddie away from me just by using words spoken against me.

We met new English friends from all over. Byron Wengard was the money (tax) collector and would make his rounds every so often. Ned's crew worked a lot in the Candlewood Lake area. One summer Saturday, the whole crew and their families went fishing at Candlewood Lake. I left Mark and Eddie with the Troyers, our neighbors, and took Dale with us. Men that Ned's crew had worked for gave us a ride on a big boat with a motor and propellers. We had a great time and caught hundreds of trout. The scariest moment on the trip happened when Molly, the oldest daughter of one of Elias's coworkers, almost fell over the boat railing and into the deep water. Molly's mother grabbed her feet just in time!

My brother Simon Jr. and Eleanor were married by now, and my brother Brian was having severe mental issues. He left the Amish for a while. Talking with him did no good. Feelings were ruined. The whole ordeal was extremely hard on Mom. At one point, no one could find Brian, but then Elias and I found him living in a neighbor's house in our territory. We went home and told Dad and Mom where he was. Mom fell to the ground—a sight I will never forget. I can still see her laying on the ground crying her poor heart out.

— 8 —

The Start

LIFE WENT ON AS USUAL for some time. Our cute baby Dean was born in May 1996. We had four boys!

Not long before Dean was born, Dad and Mom broke the news that they wanted to move and start a new settlement. We looked at different places where they could do this. They finally found 800 acres in Bergholz, Ohio, with wooded hills and valleys. You were either on the ridge or in the bottom, but you could farm in the flats. My brother, Jonas, was married to Millie Troyer by now.

My parents left Fredericktown and moved to Bergholz in the spring of 1996. All of us married children went along to help. Feelings were still ruined between Dad and my husband and others, but we helped anyway. (Dad didn't like any of his sons-in-law or daughters-in-law, and I will never know why.) Because there were no buildings on the property, they bought a trailer and moved into it until they built a big shop. The shop would have a house on one end and a barn on the other end with animals. The upstairs was the sleeping area, and they had a wash house for washing and bathing.

Before they moved, Dad and Mom had all eighteen of their children in one community with half of us married already. Moving away separated our family to the point that we couldn't talk with each other because some agreed with Dad and some didn't. I cried so much. My eyes were so swollen. I didn't want this to happen to our family. Delbert, my brother, was going steady with Marita Shrock at that time, so he stayed in Fredericktown and lived in my brother Simon Jr. and Eleanor's basement until he and Marita married. My brother Jonathan married his eighth-grade teacher, Nila Byler, leaving nine children to move to Bergholz with Dad and Mom. Since Dad's family was the only family in the new settlement, that meant no youngie, no nothing, no other families to play with for my younger siblings.

In time Dad found out that another settlement had just started in Salineville, Ohio. These people were very different. They drove yellow buggies and had storm fronts. Bonnets and mantles were brown. Ours were black. We wore shawls. They had high-heeled shoes. Their bishop, Ivan Yoder, agreed to help my dad with his settlement. It seemed suspicious to me because Ivan had just him and his children in the settlement, and Bergholz was also just my dad and his children. But the time came when both groups drove back and forth fifteen miles to church, taking turns in Bergholz one Sunday and then Salineville the next Sunday. It turned out that Ivan's daughter Ferna had a brain tumor and she had three or four children she needed help with. My younger sisters often went to Salineville to help Ferna. Being away from their Bergholz home and family was different for my sisters.

Soon after Dad left the community in Fredericktown, David Byler started a new settlement in Ulysses, Pennsylvania. My brother Jonathan had married into this family, so he left Fredericktown to go with his wife's parents to Ulysses. After the settlement started, we found out that Bishop Elmer Miller from New York wanted to visit the Bergholz church to shop around. However, the bishop met David at a bus station and David invited him to his community first. Albert agreed and stayed in Ulysses. He never visited Bergholz. I always wondered why this happened.

New Property

In the spring of 1997, Elias and I along with our four boys moved to Bergholz. We believed my dad when he said that the Fredericktown bishops were no longer working with the Bible and teaching according to Jesus's laws, so we left Fredericktown. Elias always said, "Don't put your heart in our Fredericktown house." Somehow, he knew we weren't going to stay there forever. So, I tried not to, but it was still hard for me to leave my house to another woman. Frank Yoder bought our big Fredericktown house, our ten acres, and the medium-sized barn and little shop from us for $80,000.

Across the road from Dad's place in Bergholz were sixteen acres for sale. The property had no buildings, just rocks, trees, scrub bushes, and a little woodshed. We bought this property

The Meeting

from a local real estate agent and started all over with building. In order for us to build, we had to have a huge bulldozer push stones down over the hill. At one time a brick house had been on the property, but it was falling down. People told us that the old house had had an underground passage to hide slaves. Our property also came with mineral rights, and we knew that there was coal and gas around the area, so we hoped that someday we would get paid for the gas or coal.

Before we moved to Bergholz, Elias and I and my sister Mae and Ray Jr. had plans to get a driver and go down to work on our buildings for the weekend. Then Dad and Mom dropped by with a driver from Bergholz and said we could ride down with them and Ray could come later. Elias rode in the back of the vehicle under a huge blanket with Dale, Mark, and Eddie. When we arrived in Bergholz, we phoned our driver who was going to bring us and told him we were there already. That started a huge family fight again. It almost tore the entire family apart. Ray's family was mad that we went without them. We were all crying by the time the fight was over. Big arguments and many tears! Whenever we visited Bergholz before we actually lived there, we would put up big tents and sleep in the yard or in one open upstairs with everyone else. No privacy. Those days will never be forgotten.

After living in Fredericktown for eighteen years, I rarely saw it after we moved to Bergholz. We moved Dad's empty trailer over to our property beside the woodshed and lived in there until we built a house that was pretty much the same as our Fredericktown house. Just before we moved to Bergholz, we had purchased a surrey, a two-seater buggy, which was quite different for us in the hills and mountains.

We brought with us one horse, one goat, and some chickens, so now we had to purchase grain and had no place to store it except in the shed. Of course, we soon had several raccoons wanting to eat, too. Elias shot lots of them. We also had tons of mosquitos. And talk about big spiders! I dumped a wide-mouthed can over one and the bottom was filled with legs. The body was the size of a quarter. I said that if I ever found another one, I would move back to Fredericktown. Oh, how I hated this life and thought of my big house in Fredericktown often.

While we were building our house, the little boys, now ages one-and-a-half to five, were always where Dad was. Dad let them climb high and be up on the house while he was building. To me it was too dangerous, but what could I say? Then one day it happened. Little Eddie had a ruler and was measuring one side to the next, just playing around when he backed up until he stepped off the second story and fell deep into the chimney hole that wasn't covered yet. He landed between the basement wall and the chimney wall. Elias carried him into the trailer, and luckily, he was still alive. No broken bones. He vomited a couple of times, but otherwise, he was good.

Not long before we moved to Bergholz, my brother Delbert and his wife Marita moved there. They were building down the road from us, so everyone was very busy. Family helped when they could. No one from the Fredericktown community came with us when we moved, except our brothers and sisters and their families. I was disappointed. I thought I had friends?

The Meeting

That first year we didn't have machinery, so Gregory McClain rented our field and raised corn until we were able to buy horses, plows, and other equipment. We fixed the woodshed and used it as our washhouse. We hung twine around trees to hang laundry out to dry—the second time I used twine for a clothesline. There was a path between our house and my dad's, a shortcut that we frequently used.

Across the street from us was a park-like property with nineteen acres of water, not very deep, but lots of water. We fished in the lake every year. There were always lots of Canadian geese there. They were like watchdogs—"Honk, honk, honk!"—whenever someone came near them.

Another piece of property, which my dad owned, was attached to our sixteen acres. Dad was asking $500 an acre for forty acres of field and pasture and forty acres of woodland. We paid him $40,000 for those eighty acres, and we paid the full tax on that piece of land ever since we had moved to Bergholz. After we paid Dad for the property, he wouldn't give us the deed. I'll never forget how I cried because he had our money plus he had the deed. Who wants to pay for property and not own it? I heard him say "No deed," which was very wrong and sure didn't help feelings at all. It only made things worse.

We attended church in Salineville or Bergholz. It was a nice buggy ride on Sunday mornings when the sun was shining! Sometimes we went over a back road over to Salineville and passed donkeys. The children would always enjoy seeing them.

Our daughter Eve was born in December 1997 in our basement. We were thrilled! My first girl. She had a touch of cholic... it was bad enough.

Amish Ways

One of our new neighbors gave the whole family mouth harps to blow in. They used to be a NO-NO with Dad. But now, they were okay again? Dad was also allowing the ones that moved down with them (my brother and sister) more things than we were ever allowed to have or do, which caused more bitter feelings. When I asked about their freedoms, Dad answered me with "Because they listened to me." Oh! I always listened to you, too! What a lame excuse. Why was it that I always picked up on these things? It just made me feel bad. My first gift from Elias had been a harp. I had to give it back. Why? Just a Dad rule!

The Amish religion was always "If you leave the Amish, you'll be shunned"—Amish laws, not Bible laws. As I write about my life, lots of questions go through my mind like "Why can Amish ride in vans, but they would be punished if they drove one?" Nobody can answer my questions. The Amish life, to me, is so confusing. I spent lots of years confused, although I felt when I married Elias that he put me in chains and shackles and threw me into a dungeon of darkness while he lived happily and did what he wanted to do. What could I do? I was helpless. No one would believe me if I told them and I knew I'd be punished if I did tell. Not physically punished; spiritually I was locked up.

My dad and Elias sure hadn't changed toward each other yet,

The Meeting

nor had things changed between Elias and his dad, which was confusing for me. So many confusing feelings. Memories of my home life are work, work, work from dawn until dusk, always. Dad and Mom, brothers and sisters, never said "Thank you" or "I love you!" Amish don't do that. You owe them work. No pay except one dollar here or there. They believe that if you pay someone money, they will buy things like cigarettes or a stereo. Nobody trusts anybody.

In 1994 after Eddie was born, my health deteriorated with a bad case of arthritis, and I was in a wheelchair. I was miserable. Visitors came by to see me, and most wished me well for the future, but one of my friends said to me, "Maybe God wants you like this. You just have to accept it." I was heartbroken. I went on a fruit and vegetable diet with herbs and vitamins and one aspirin every time I took herbs. Finally, I got better, but my arthritis never went completely away.

Amish life looks good, a nice painted picture, but the inside is hollow. This is my view. Someone else might not say that. I was always searching for something more fulfilling. I thought that once I had a sweetheart, someone to love, children of my own, it would be better. But no, Elias didn't fill that void in my heart. He made it worse. For some reason, I had it in my mind that someday I would be set free and diamonds and pearls would be mine. I always had that precious diamond in my mind and searched for love. But I felt that God had left me completely. Why, oh why, God? Later in my story, you will see why I searched for a different life.

Part 3
Bergholz

–9–

The Community

IT IS NOW 2005. BERGHOLZ has twenty to twenty-five families, and our family is growing, too. Elias Jr., Stephen, Alexander, Ivan, and Jeremy joined our family. We ended up with nine boys and one girl.

Back in 1998, Elias had started his own carpentry crew. However, he had a bad thing going on in his life: flirting with women he built for and telling me their names. With that attitude, he shot arrows into my heart every time. Although I hurt terribly inside, I made excuses for him. I told myself that I would be satisfied with Elias and somehow do the best I could because every man is a man and every man has a bad habit of some kind that I wouldn't like. I also told myself that if I couldn't love Elias, I couldn't love anyone. So, I made the best of it. I didn't know if that was true—just my thoughts.

Elias had told me on the night of our marriage that my job

would be giving birth to children and staying inside the house to clean, take care of the children, and cook. So, for over twenty years I had no idea what the world was like around me. I could not make a call with a phone, never had money, and didn't do a checkbook a lot of times. I had no idea how much money we had. Elias would do all those things, and he also picked up the groceries, so I seldom went outside the house. We went to my folks on Sundays, but we were mostly inside their house. I felt like I was captured with chains on my arms and shackles on my legs and was thrown into the darkness of misery. I was very lonely and sad. I asked myself many times if I would ever be released somehow from my situation. Nobody knows this because I wouldn't tell anyone. Elias wasn't like this when we were seeing each other. He made me believe that he would be a farmer, so I was deceived in many ways. I thought I'd married a good Amish Christian. I was disappointed and confused. Behind those closed doors, life was black and dark.

Now we had church every two weeks with my dad, Simon Mullet, as bishop, Jonas Mullet and Leon Miller as ministers, and Lawrence Troyer as the deacon. All were anointed here in Bergholz. We re-connected with Fredericktown churches, Ashland churches, and others, but a lot of times could tell and feel that we weren't welcomed back although people would say they were happy to see us again. I usually asked myself, "Why, oh, why did people not accept Dad? Why was he so different?" Dad always told me that it was because he was living a righteous life. Why did I not believe my dad? I didn't know any different. Amish churches where I was born and raised always had fights to settle. I would get so upset and bored. The things they fought about had nothing to do with Jesus. Why couldn't they see it that way? Why? Would I always have these thoughts? Would there ever be answers?

Family

Elias's parents, the Martin Shrocks, left Ashland and moved to Bergholz along with Elias's brother Silas and family, the Jon Troyers, the Lawrence Troyers, and the Johnny Troyers. My sister Winnie married Adam Troyer, and my sister Norma married Alvin Yoder. Another sister Bethany married Joseph Yoder, and Abigail married Uriah Yoder. Lucille, another one of my sisters, married Fredrick Miller. Other families in our community included the Leon Millers, Leroy Millers, and Able Miller who got himself a girlfriend here from Pennsylvania. Matthew Miller's son Randall and Leon Miller's daughter Karen married in Bergholz. Leon Miller was not related to the other Millers. Leroy, Able, Ed, Randall, and Mervin Miller were all brothers. (Mervin also moved to our community.) The Miller boys' sister Nellie married Forrest Burkholder. I know that's a lot of names, but these people all play an important role in the future of the Bergholz community.

My sister Emily, who married Edgar Hostetler from Pennsylvania, became extremely ill with pancreatic liver cancer after the birth of their firstborn, Lana. Emily was very yellow—jaundiced. She had two more children, Emily and little Jordan, after her sickness began. Jordan was raised by my parents because

Emily was too sick to take care of him. She had an operation to remove half of her insides and replace them with plastic tubes. After the surgery, her weight dropped to ninety pounds, and she was still very yellow. We spent many days taking turns going to the hospital to visit or stay. Later she came home and brought her IV monitor home with her, but she died on August 10, 2003. Nobody will ever know how I missed her. She was like me. We were very close, and I loved her dearly. A part of me went with her. From what Dad told me, Edgar was not nice to her either, but I did not know much about their everyday life. Later, Edgar met Norah Byler from Pennsylvania. She was a single schoolteacher and eventually they were married. Norah took Edgar and Emily's children and loved them and treated them like they were her own. We were incredibly happy about that, and I secretly prayed for her. They moved to Edgar's house on top of the hill.

My brother Elmer loved horses and shod them for other people. I secretly loved my brother Elmer more than my other siblings. We were so much alike. Nobody knew but us. I loved all my siblings, don't get me wrong, except Maggie, my oldest sister. She and I had problems. She hated me and threw things against me to make it look bad for me. Even as we were older, she came between our children. But in later years, our relationship would be fixed very differently than we ever expected it to be.

One Christmas I was gathering presents together for my children when my brother Simon Jr. and his wife Eleanor visited us. I saw that they had a little toy chainsaw that sounded like it was cutting a log when you pulled the rope. I asked Eleanor where she got it and she told the Dollar Tree store. Since I had already gotten my groceries, I didn't want to make a trip to town to get a chainsaw before Christmas. I found out that my brother Jonas's wife Millie was making a trip to town, so I asked her to stop and get a chainsaw for me and she said that she would. When she came back, she said that only two were left and since she didn't have anything for her boys yet, she decided to keep them. She needed two so her boys wouldn't fight. Talk about a let-down. She said she wouldn't have known about them if I hadn't told her. The same thing happened with my brother Elmer's wife Nora. I asked her to get me a little stroller with one seat and two little handles so it would be easier to push and my boys could push the baby around. The stroller itself was heavy. She said she would get the stroller, but the same thing happened. She bought two and said she needed them for her children! I was crushed. Don't tell me you will if you won't give it to me.

– 10 –

Trouble Begins

IN 2005, CHURCH PROBLEMS STARTED happening more often. We found out that Lawrence Troyer's family was getting into trouble more and more. They did little things like ordering strings to help their boys build a guitar. Amish can sing but not have instruments of any sort. A lot more things happened with them being involved in smaller things which ended up as bigger things. Things worsened until the church had to shun both Lawrence and his wife. My dad said it was a six-month ban (shun) until they repented.

My sister Winnie's boyfriend Adam, Lawrence's son, was working for a logger and made a huge mistake. Adam had bought trees on some property, but he paid the renter instead of the landowner for the trees. The renter took the money and left, so Adam was put in jail. Since Adam and Winnie were dating at the time, Dad went and brought him home. Adam's sister Valerie was dating my brother Chester at the time, and Valerie was almost frantic over Adam being in jail. (After Adam and Winnie were married, baby Martha was born. They lived on top of Mooretown Hill in a house that was built inground behind huge pine trees. A shed was located across the drive.)

After my dad shunned Lawrence and his wife, they ended up selling all their machinery, leaving Bergholz, and moving to Ulysses, Pennsylvania. Bishop Albert Miller thought they were unjustly shunned and took them out of shunning. They even had a special church meeting during the week where three hundred bishops and ministers from around the Amish communities came to an agreement to overturn the Bergholz shunning and allow the Troyers in their churches. Now they were free, and the Amish all turned against Bergholz. Simon's shunning fell on himself and his church.

Next, the Martin Shrocks, Elias's family, started getting in trouble. They promised to help build up our church, but they wanted new and different things, more modern. They wanted things like musical clocks. Then Silas built a shop for mechanic repair. He put skylights in the roof even though he knew he wasn't supposed to. He also had solar panels to charge his battery—also against the church rules. One thing followed another until we had to shun them to keep new things from coming into the walls of our church. Now "people" started saying that just because Martin didn't agree with my dad Simon, Simon shunned Martin. They claimed that Simon didn't like Martin. This was not true. Martin was shunned for trying to bring new things into the church. Martin had a background of disagreeing with every church he was in and causing problems. He could have gone to my dad's house during the week to discuss his problems, but he always waited until Sunday morning. Martin, Simon (our bishop), and the ministers would stand out in the barn and argue, sometimes yelling so loudly that we could hear them in the house. Women and children were waiting patiently; babies were crying. It was very annoying. So, Martin was shunned. His wife, Arlene, didn't want to leave him after all the years they'd been together, so she took his side just to be with him and was shunned, too. All Martin's children living in Bergholz took his side except Elias who stuck with me and separated from his family.

In 2007, Martin and his children left Bergholz. Martin and Arlene moved to Fredericktown. Stephen's family moved to Ashland. James Stutzman moved to Stanwood, Michigan. After Martin moved, they came down to be with Silas's family until they could move to Stanwood. Elias's sister Susan had married Bernie Keim from Ashland while in Bergholz, and they moved to New York right after the wedding. Dan married Elsie from Ulysses, and because she was Bishop Albert Miller's daughter, Dan moved to Ulysses. Elias's sister Sara and her husband Joseph Wengard remained in Ashland, having never moved to Bergholz. Also, Ivan's Raymond was the only one left. Rachel and her husband Alan had previously moved to Ulysses. So now the Shrock family was scattered all over.

My brother Brian and his wife Ruthann lived in Bergholz, as well, but in 1999 they left. They had been married while we lived in Fredericktown. Ruthann's real name was Terry, but Dad and Mom gave her an Amish name, Ruthann, when they moved to Bergholz. Brian and Ruthann were English and had a family when they came back. Ruthann was willing to change her name and come along with Brian to be Amish. Brian had an extremely hard and complicated life. He and Ruthann came and went, English then Amish, back and forth. We never knew when they'd take off or come back.

The members of the Bergholz community continuously went to the Mount Hope and Kidron, Ohio, machinery sales and always got into arguments with others, sometimes to the point that the police had to be involved. The Bergholz community hasn't had visitors from other communities since 2005—a long time. As of today, still no visitors. If someone tries to talk to them, they refuse. They teach everyone in the community to stay away from kind people because kind people are dangerous and will kill your spirit. They also teach people that if you step outside Bergholz walls, you will go to hell.

— 11 —

The Devil

ABOUT THE SAME TIME THE problems happened with the Troyers and the Shrocks, my brother Elmer was possessed by the devil so badly that he was a living soul walking and talking like the devil. You could see the devil plainly on Elmer's face. He spoke many things about our church. He said things were going on behind closed doors that no one knew about. I felt that God let him do this to show us how the devil acts. The whole situation reminded me of the Bible story about Aaron. Something was wrong. Very wrong.

Elmer would throw himself on the ground on his back with a loud thud. Then he'd get back up and say, "If I'm Elmer, I will stand here. If I'm the devil, I will fall on the ground." Instantly, he would fall to the ground on his back. I didn't see him do this personally, but it sounded scary.

One day Elmer said that his baby girl Samantha was not his child. He insisted on knowing whose baby she was. Then he started going from baby to baby trying to find the right one. We didn't know what to do about it or why he would say something like that. Finally, I told him I wanted to help him with his life. To help Elmer feel better and be at peace, Elias and I took him and his daughter Samantha to Steubenville for a DNA test. When the papers came back, my dad said they read "A close related kin . . . as brother, etc." Dad said it didn't say who the father was, so we had spent six hundred dollars for nothing. I did not read the papers, so maybe my dad lied?

Elmer had to be watched all the time and not left alone. Some of the people in our community were too scared to come help with him, but one night the Miller boys sat with him. I don't remember what all was said, but Elmer stood up and whacked Leroy Miller in the face cutting his tongue and lips.

Another time during the day, when Elmer was at his worst, we were all told to leave, and Dad stayed with Elmer. Norah and the children were in the bedroom while Dad and Elmer argued and fought back and forth. Norah was scared, so she crawled out the window with her girls and walked up to Dad's house.

Dad said he kept looking out the window for help, but no one showed up. He had to deal with Elmer alone. According to Dad, the devil showed himself plain as day on Elmer's face. He intended to kill Dad, but Dad's life was spared. Elmer ended up on the floor in a bad sweat and he screamed like Dad said he'd never heard before, causing chills to run up and down his spine. The whole situation was scary. After that, Dad left Elmer and went home. Soon Elmer found his way up to the farm. (Later that night I found out that Elmer had been at school, scared the children, and looked awful.) Elmer hung around Dad's phone shack and kept saying, "Our situation is going to be phoned real fast all over the world. People have phones; our story will be spread worldwide." I can still see the look on his face.

That night, Elias and I went over to Dad's and left our children at home. I was sitting in the living room on the couch closest to the door. Suddenly, the door opened, and Elmer walked in. I could not see his eyes, but I said, "Dad, he's here!" He was standing beside the desk, arms behind his back.

Dad stood up, walked over to Elmer, and said, "Come on, Elmer. Just settle down, please."

Elmer got so mad. He had a cane behind his back to hit Dad with, but Dad stopped him. Then Elmer grabbed a gun, pointed it at Dad, and pulled the trigger. But, there was no bullet. Dad grabbed the gun, and the fight was on. Elmer yanked a big handful of hair out of Dad's beard.

I spoke up and said to Mom and my brother Jonas "That's enough. You've got to lock him up! Enough is enough. Someone is going to get killed." So, Elias went to call the ambulance.

When the ambulance showed up, Dad and Elmer parted from each other. Elmer said, "Huh! I have help now" and asked the ambulance guys for a gun. They weren't allowed to touch him until they heard him threaten someone. At that point, they grabbed him, handcuffed him, and took him to the hospital. An hour later, Elmer's donkey, which was out in his barn, yelled so loud we all heard it at Dad's house. (Dad didn't want Elmer to have a donkey.) It was like the donkey knew his master was being taken away. The real reason Elmer lashed out at Dad was that Elmer found out Dad had been flirting with Nora, Elmer's wife. Elmer was angry because Dad was trying to sleep with Nora.

Before Elmer went to the hospital, he was showing the rest of us how hard it was to change a bad spirit of a person into a good spirit. It does not happen overnight at all. After he left, life continued, but what people witnessed changed their lives. We realized we weren't living according to the Bible. The whole church started repenting from sin and turned their lives around. Others fled for their lives. We wanted to change and fix our lives, so we started confessing sins to the church, which was the right thing to do according to the Amish.

People started cleaning up their houses. My sisters still living at home—Norma, Winnie, Bethany, Abigail, and Lucille—had rooms that were too "fancy." They took miscellaneous items off the walls; my brother Levi threw catalogs away which had a great hold on him. Repent! Repent! I didn't have anything to throw away. I had my hands full with the children, so I never had a chance to have a lot of pictures and things hanging or standing around. Many others did. My mom had piles and piles to discard. She had a keychain trinket collection and she liked toys. Sometimes the kids were allowed to play with her collection, but she mostly kept it for herself. She also collected children's books and had lots and lots—drawers full. She got rid of most of them. She also had too many dishes standing around. She thought she had too much pride in them so lots of them were sold. The cushions on the rocking chairs were too fancy as well, so they were thrown out, and Mom put simple cushions with no backs on the chairs.

— 12 —

Confessions

MY SISTER WINNIE AND HER husband Adam were having marriage problems. Adam wanted to move with his mom and dad to Ulysses, but Winnie didn't want to go. We knew something more was going on between them, but no one knew what. So, we kept a good watch. One day while Adam was at work, Winnie talked to Dad and then to Elmer, my brother. She admitted that Adam had been sexually abusing her. I won't share the details, but the abuse was very bad. When Adam came home from work, Elmer met him by the door and chased him home. We kept Winnie and little Martha safe at my dad's house.

The day that Winnie told Dad and Elmer about Adam is when big trouble began!!! Not everybody agreed with what was happening—"Amish don't take this action, just the English do." Bergholz was in trouble. What the Bible says came out real fast, and big arguments started. While some say you can't tear apart what God put together, Bergholz says in smaller words in the exact same verse that if you're caught in deep sin, you can part.

Adam wrote a letter confessing a deep sin he was caught in. He said he wrote the letter because my dad promised him he would get Winnie and little Martha back if he wrote it. Winnie wrote an identical letter, but they didn't get back together. Winnie said it was just like God had opened her eyes and put a book in front of her and showed her Adam's whole life and everything he had done from his young years until they were married—deep sins that pulled them apart. Winnie believed it, but Adam didn't. (This story about Adam and Winnie will become clearer later.)

Somehow, Winnie went back to Adam for a little while. One evening, Lawrence stopped by with intentions to load up Adam, Winnie, and little Martha and take them to Ulysses! Winnie escaped and ran upstairs, lit a lamp, put her head between her knees, and started praying hard for help from home. My dad had no idea what was going on but decided to take some of my brothers to check on Winnie and Adam. When they arrived, they found the Lawrence Troyers in Winnie's house. Surprise!

Elmer, who was quite mad that Adam's family was there, planned to walk in first, but he said our brother Leroy grabbed him by the pant belt, pulled him back, and said, "Let the leaders go first." Dad went in and stopped the Lawrences from taking Adam and Winnie. Jon Troyer was there, too, and was pushed hard by one of the fellows and fell. He soon left. Then Lawrence's Marie had little Martha, heading for the van. Dad stopped her and took Martha back to Winnie. After that, the Troyers all left, or so we thought. Adam talked like he was on Winnie's side so everyone, including Adam and Winnie, went to Dad's house until bedtime.

The next day Adam was incredibly angry. He had planned to get up in the middle of the night and leave, but he slept so hard he didn't wake up until it was too late. Maybe that was what separated them? Adam was kicked out of my dad's house, and he went home. Adam said he lay on his back that night on the driveway and looked toward the starry sky and prayed to God that, if it were God's will, he and Winnie would get back together again. Life continued until . . .

Dad decided that Adam should go to Ulysses to repent of his sins to Bishop Albert Miller. So, Dad, Mom, Winnie, little Martha, Johnny and Millie, Leon, Elmer and Nora, and Elias and I hired a van and driver, picked up Adam, and drove him to Ulysses. Adam, not knowing what was going on, stood there in front of us and repented of his deep sin to Albert. We all heard him say it. Then we drove him to Lawrence's and did the same thing. We stood in a circle in front of Lawrence, and Adam repeated what he did. He also convinced his mom to agree that what he said was true. My dad told Adam, "Fix your life and stop doing what you did and then come back to get your family." After that, we left Adam and his bags there and went home to Bergholz. Elias asked Leon if there was any way Adam could slip out of this situation, and Leon replied, "There is always a way. We shall see."

Dad also told Adam that he could have all the things in the house and the barn because Winnie was going back home with her parents. Winnie went to the house to get some clothes, discovered the furniture gone, and thought that the stuff had been stolen. What a mess!

Later, we found out that Adam took back his confession, saying the only reason he said what he did was because Dad promised him that he could get Winnie back. He also claimed the letter he wrote wasn't true and my dad had told him what to write on the paper. Oh me, oh my! Here we go!

With everything happening with the shunning and confessions, some in the community felt scared and left. People came from Ashland and loaded up Jon Troyer, Jerry Troyer, and their families. After everything was loaded, their cars wouldn't start. Then a man was standing outside a semi and how he was standing made it look like he was shooting an arrow into the sky. Seeing him made a chill go down my spine. I wondered if an angel was helping them escape the Bergholz Amish Community.

I had a very sad, sinking feeling when the Jon Troyer family left. The family was shunned because Jon said he agreed with Martin Shrock. Lightning struck again. Jon's family was being separated. Four of his children stayed in Bergholz, and it couldn't be fixed—all just because of choices people made. What's done is done.

One Sunday before Jon Yoder and his family left, my brother Elmer, Nora, Elias, and I went to see them along with Alvin and Norma. When we drove in their drive, Jon was sitting in his chair, his head laid back, the color on his face white and pink like death. He looked dead, and it felt like it does at a funeral.

Time moves on. Winnie is living at Dad's house with little Martha and is pregnant with another child while Adam is living with his parents, the Lawrence Troyers, in Ulysses, PA. When school started, Winnie needed income, so she taught school and Martha stayed with Dad. Winnie would go to the Kidron Clinic for check-ups, and Adam found out about it. So, he loaded up some friends in a van, sat down the road from the clinic, and sent his friend Enoch into the clinic to talk to Winnie and persuade her to come to the van. The police were called, and they asked Winnie if she wanted to talk to Adam or not. She told them no, so the police made Adam's van leave.

In early December 2006 baby Lily was born. Because of the situation with Adam, the birthing center gave Winnie a code to share with only those she wanted to visit. Afterward, she came to Bergholz, safe with her two little girls. She continued to teach school while the girls stayed at Dad's.

Adam and Winnie sent letters to each other and occasionally they sent cards. Everyone looked at the letters and cards, read them, and said what they thought of them. Passing the letters around was my dad's way of knowing if someone was on his side or not. We would have to say how we felt or express ourselves. Dad made us talk to him time and again and tell him everything we knew, so he could tell us what to do and why to do it. Whoever went against him was punished. The punishment started out with the person staying in their own home, not talking to anyone else, so no one fell into the same way of thinking. This always caused a meeting where we discussed who was on whose side. Women gathered in circles and talked making sure we were on the same page so no problems occurred.

Separation

One fine, beautiful Monday morning, Sheriff Frank Abrams drove up the drive and asked to talk to Winnie. Dad was at the Carrollton auction, and Mom didn't want Winnie to talk, but Frank put his hand on Winnie's shoulder and asked to speak with her alone outside so they could talk freely. Frank said, "Adam still loves you. Do you want to see him?" It was obvious that she wanted to go and be with Adam because the sheriff did not force her to go—it was her choice. She went with the sheriff to the car and sent Abigail and Lucille inside to get the girls for her. Frank drove her to Somerset Road where Adam was waiting with my brothers Simon Jr. and Jonathan and my sister Mae. They wanted to go to Indiana and counsel with Winnie, who agreed.

When Dad arrived home, he called Sheriff Frank, who told him that Winnie was fine. To ease Dad's mind, Frank called Winnie and let Dad speak with her. Frank told Dad that he had given Winnie his number in case she wanted to come back. Frank also made Adam promise that he wouldn't take Winnie to Ulysses. No family members from either side were allowed to visit, but alas, Lawrence and Marie, Adam's parents, showed up in Indiana.

Without a teacher, our Amish school shut down, and the remaining eighteen families in Bergholz gathered at Dad's house to stay 24/7. Dad thought everything happened with Winnie because all of us were living in sin. We started straightening up lives again so we could get her and the girls back. Lights were kept on 24/7, and we took turns sitting up all night. We only went home to wash clothes, gather things we needed, and do chores. We set up big tables in the kitchen like wedding tables for everyone to eat at. We fixed the food in the daytime, cleaned and did laundry, and made midnight snacks. However, some of us were given different jobs and assignments. At the time, I was pregnant and sick, and since I was chosen to be Dad's righthand maid, I was permitted to sit and talk in the ring beside Dad. I didn't help with the work, which caused lots of problems—jealousy, hate, and fights against each other. We always tried our best to work together, but every now and then, there were adult fights to settle.

In the meantime, I knew my marriage with Elias was messed up, too. So, I said, "If Winnie can't be with Adam, I can't be with Elias." And just like that, Elias and I separated. I stayed with the group at Dad's and Elias went home. We were separated for a total of eight weeks. What a life. Because I had no communication with Elias, life became a nightmare after not being apart during our eighteen years of marriage! For many hours I cried so hard from the bottom of my stomach that it felt like my insides were falling out. The others could hear me outside and occasionally came to sit with me. I felt so alone, especially with the kids. Nobody can help better than a parent who knows his child. After a few weeks, I was permitted to talk to Elias for fifteen minutes at a time. While Elias and I lived separately, other couples started to separate, and a lot of them thought they helped their marriage by just staying away for a while.

Since I was being protected by my dad, I sat with him in the yard around the circle whenever I felt able to. I kept teaching the

Betrayed and Rejected

others how they had to follow in my dad's footsteps. One of the things I told the others was to lie about all things that they heard and saw him do. Lying was the only way. That bothered me a lot because I hate lies and was always told not to lie. Both of my parents and God taught me not to lie! But let me say this again: The ONLY way a person can understand my dad's language is to lie about what he says and his actions.

After five or six weeks we received a letter from Winnie asking us to pick her up at my brother Jonathan's house in Ulysses! So... Adam did take Winnie to Ulysses after he was warned not to by the sheriff! Dad chose five people—my brother Elmer, Ed Miller, my sisters Abigail and Lucille, and myself—to make the five-and-a-half-hour trip to Pennsylvania to bring Winnie home. When we arrived, we stopped at Jonathan's house only to find a note on the door saying "I changed my mind." We went inside to Winnie's room and found a bag partly packed with some of Adam and Winnie's belongings. It looked like they were both coming back home. The baby's car seat was on the bed.

Not knowing what else to do, we drove over to Adam's parents' house. Of course, all the doors were locked, and no one answered the door. We looked all around the house, and Abigail said she thought she saw an arm in the window and heard someone cry. This was too much for Brother Elmer. He pushed open a window and crawled inside while the rest of us stood outside to watch if someone fled out the back door. When we heard loud voices inside, Abigail also went in through the window while Lucille and Ed went through the door. I was left alone to watch outside.

Bergholz

Suddenly, Alvin Troyer went running across the yard as fast as he could go to the neighbors. Within minutes, both driveways were blocked by other vehicles, and we were captured by our enemies. We had driven right into a trap.

By this point, Brother Elmer had gone upstairs and met Lawrence at the top of the stairs. Elmer yelled, "Where is my sister?" Lawrence said that she went fishing with Adam, but he wouldn't tell Elmer where they went. Lawrence and Elmer continued yelling at each other about the past when Lawrence and his family had lived in Bergholz. Their faces were close together as they yelled back and forth. Elmer said Lawrence's beard was awful close, and that was too much for Elmer! He grabbed Lawrence's beard and held it tight as they stared at each other.

Alvin Troyer came back saying that he had called the police and we were all under arrest. When the police arrived, we had to leave the house. The Troyers stood on one side of the yard and the Bergholz group on the other while the police listened to the story. My brother Elmer and Ed Miller were handcuffed and forced to sit in the yard. There we waited for a couple of hours under the watchful eye of a police officer. It was all we could do to not panic.

Elmer talked about everything and anything to the police to break the silence. One conversation Elmer started was about how Christians treat their friends. Lawrence said, "Treat others the way you want to be treated." Then he turned around, called the police, and signed the papers to arrest and press charges against his friends. We were like "WOW, so that's how you want people to treat you!?"

Finally, the police put Elmer in one police car and Ed in another to separate them. The police couldn't decide right away which one wanted to take Elmer because he wouldn't shut up. He kept talking about treating your neighbor as you want to be treated, plus he was a little wild in handcuffs. We ladies went with our driver back into town to have a hearing before a judge at two o'clock in the morning. The judge sentenced both Elmer and Ed to jail and sent the rest of us back to Ohio, leaving our two "bodyguards" there in jail and without seeing Winnie. I looked at Ed and asked, "Will Louisa (his wife) be all right?" He smiled and said, "Yes."

After the sentencing, we went to the police station to talk to Elmer and Ed before we left and to see if we could talk to Winnie. Well, they separated them, and the police officer talked to Winnie and then to Adam. The officer told us Winnie didn't want to see us or go home with us. We were devastated and disappointed that we got into this mess because of her. Abigail, Lucille, and I begged the police to let us talk to her, but because she refused, we had to leave. We called home before we left Ulysses to let everyone know what had happened.

My two sisters and I arrived at my dad's house late that afternoon. We were exhausted. Everything looked too bleak and dark. To make matters worse, Elias and I were still separated, my kids were all at Dad's house, and it was Sunday. Everybody there was dressed in clean Sunday clothes except my children. They'd had no bath on Saturday and were in dirty clothes—neglected. As tired as I was, I had to wash the kids. I sent the older ones to our home to get clean clothes. Even though I had been chosen to go after Winnie and left all my kids at Dad's, no one looked after them. This cut me deeply! The community wanted my help but ignored my ten beautiful kids—nine boys and one girl. Elias had been at home alone the whole time. Why didn't they take my kids home to Elias? He would have bathed them and put clean clothes on them.

Dad and my brother Jonas went to the Pennsylvania jailhouse to pay the bond and bring Elmer and Ed home. Well, they bailed them out, but Dad and Elmer got into an argument on the way home. The tension was great. Dad said that he wished he had left Elmer in jail.

Next came the court trial before the judge to determine who was guilty. A whole van load went along—Elmer's wife Nora, Ed Miller's wife Louisa, Abigail, Lucille, Dad, Mom, and me. We walked into the courtroom and talked to our lawyer, Byrun Felmuth. Winnie was not there at the time, but she was supposed to go on the witness stand to testify since everything was about her.

Lawrence went on the stand under oath, promising to tell the truth with his hand on the Bible. One of the first questions asked was about how Elmer had grabbed Lawrence's beard. Lawrence said that Elmer grabbed him by the throat! WHAT? We started talking while court was in session ... OMG! Such a lie! The judge made us be quiet. The rest of the hearing continued with the usual questions.

Suddenly, the door opened, and Winnie entered. She could barely walk. We were all shocked! She had gained a lot of weight, and her legs and feet were swollen badly. When it was Winnie's turn on the stand, the lady doing the oath went over to help Winnie to her feet and walk her to the stand. Winnie did the same thing as Lawrence—promised under oath to tell the truth with her hand on the Bible. When she was asked about the letter she wrote home, she said she didn't feel that way anymore. I knew she was lying. No one would write such a letter to her family to come and get her and then say it wasn't true. What she told her parents was another lie.

After the witnesses finished, we were dismissed from the courtroom, and Winnie left to find Adam. Abigail and Lucille asked the lawyer if they could talk to Winnie outside the court before she left, and he said, "Yes." The girls and I ran outside and caught up to Winnie on the walkway. We started talking, and she was hesitant at first, but then started talking. Adam was there instantly to protect her. Long story short, we discussed a lot and begged her to come home. Adam started sweating like a dog because I think he realized he was losing Winnie. Abigail, Lucille, and I worked hard and finally convinced Winnie to come home with us. She agreed, and we took a different route home so no one could trail us or stop us.

With Winnie back in Bergholz, everyone went home after seven weeks of living in my parents' home. Elias and I were back together—a weird, funny feeling—but it didn't take long until I realized nothing had changed. Elias was still the same. We had been separated for eight weeks and nothing had been accomplished. Everything was still the same. Life went on as usual.

— 13 —

Punishment

After Winnie came home, Dad told us all that we were not living righteous lives or else none of those things would have happened. If I may say how I feel, I think it was Dad that wasn't living a righteous life, not the church people, but nobody was allowed to stand up and disagree with Dad. If you did, there was a punishment to follow.

To help us live better, we started with punishments for known problems. First, Richard Byler put Leon Miller in the chicken coop in the barn. He gave Leon blankets and clothes and took him food for every meal. Leon had an extreme temper. He would throw hammers at the children and kick them unnecessarily. One time one of his horses got out, and Leon shot and accidentally killed the horse. He couldn't control himself. Leon's temper was the main reason he was separated from his family for a while. The hope was that the separation would make him realize he was in the wrong and needed to treat his family better. At one point, Leon disobeyed Richard, so Richard drug Leon through horse manure and cut off Leon's beard. (This is where the beard-cutting started.) Leon admitted that he thought these things would help him to overcome his anger. And so, the punishments began.

On Sundays after church, we sat in a circle, confessed sins to each other, and took punishments. To help with the punishments, my brother-in-law Edgar created a big wooden paddle with twenty holes in it. My mom took whippings with the paddle because she was turning her own children against each other behind our backs. She would talk to me about my sister Maggie and talk to Maggie about me. It reached the point that Maggie and I couldn't even talk to each other. Maggie had wanted a huge family, but she only had six children while I had ten. My having more children caused a lot of jealousy and resentment. And then, Mom admitted to telling Maggie her children were not as cute as mine, and naturally, Maggie was offended. I had no clue any of this was happening and couldn't understand why Maggie and I couldn't talk to each other anymore. Before we had kids, we always talked about life. So, because Mom purposely tried to cause ill feelings between her children (she did the same thing to several of the other kids), she was spanked.

Most of the men admitted to having sexual thoughts about women in the church other than their own wives. Lusting over another man's wife was a huge problem! So, most of the men were spanked for lusting after other women and for saying bad things about them. I was called a "blue-legged b***h" by the

Miller boys, Able and Mervin. One after another, men were put in the chicken coops.

Because Elias lusted after not only church women, but also women of the world, he was pitched in with the billy goat in the barn. He wasn't allowed in the house and lived strictly in the barn for two weeks. The first night Elias was in the barn, Dad sent my brother Chester over to check on Elias. Elias had no clue that anyone was near the barn, so when he heard noises outside, he grabbed a broom and waited by the door. Chester approached the barn and had his pants open. Elias started beating the crap out of Chester. One other time when Elias and Chester were wrestling at Dad's house, Elias managed to get his finger caught in the buttonhole of Chester's pants and rip them open far and wide. Chester stood there and literally said, "Beat me, Elias! As you beat me, you are beating Jesus Christ." Elias didn't care whom he beat and told Chester to LEAVE! (This incident made my dad think maybe Elias was gay. Elias said the reason he ripped open Chester's pants was because Chester was trying to make it look like he wasn't gay anymore and Elias knew that wasn't true. Why couldn't Dad ever just take things the way they were instead of always switching things around to something else?)

The next Sunday, everyone, including Dad, agreed that now that Elias had the privilege of beating up Chester it was now Chester's turn to beat up Elias in front of everyone. Chester took an ax handle, went back to the corn crib, and beat the crap out of Elias. Elias fought back until he couldn't anymore because he was surrounded by all the church men. Then Chester brought

Elias into the house, made him bend down in front of the other women and me, and used the ax handle on him. Elias squirmed and wiggled trying to get away, but a man stood on each side so he couldn't escape. It was horrible.

Finally, my brother Jonas spoke up and made Chester stop. A couple more whacks could have easily broken Elias's spine or killed him. All this time, Dad sat in a chair watching and not saying anything. Then Dad told me that I must make Elias sleep on the floor in the living room with no blankets. I disobeyed and told Elias to lay on the couch. His whole body was black and blue, plus he was shaking. I gave him blankets and pillows. I believed in punishing, but this was beyond punishing. It was cruelty.

After Dad wondered about Elias being gay, Chester confessed in church that he was having sex with the Troyer boys and had sex with a minor Troyer girl when the girl had gone to the garden alone to get vegetables for a meal. I found out that Chester, who always signed his name as "A Soldier in God's Army," repented from his sin because he figured, if he confessed, the Troyer children would get in trouble. However, Chester was the adult, and the Troyer children were minors. Because Chester confessed only to get others in trouble, he could not be healed, he will never be forgiven, and he would be tagged on his forehead with the words "child molester" that can never be erased. As a result of his confession, Chester was arrested and placed on probation for twenty-five years, and he is now a registered sex offender.

Ed Miller was sent to the chicken coop because he confessed to walking up to a woman in Walmart and telling her he liked her boobs. Then Victor went into the chicken coop for lusting. Leroy Miller went for not providing for his family and not being the man of the house. After Elias's barn incident, he also now goes into the coop. Everyone admitted that the punishments were helping their lives. In the meantime, kids were going to school as usual, and my dad was giving the ladies money to survive on.

Then Ed Miller left the coop without being told. He said he was so cold and couldn't take it anymore, but Dad convinced him to go back. Because Ed had walked out, Randel took his blanket away from him and spanked him hard with the huge paddle. The temperature outside was below zero, and because Ed had no blankets and just a coat for warmth, he had to walk in circles to keep warm. If he sat down, he would freeze to death. Ed was told by my dad to write his life's story—everything he and Louisa had ever done while dating and after marriage. Ed made sure he wrote every little detail because he was freezing and wanted out of the coop. Then Dad told him to write everything twice. (Later, you will see why Dad wanted Ed to write all the details twice.)

Forcing people to share all about their sex lives with the whole church was devastating. Men wrote letters to Dad confessing sins, and Dad handed the letters to everyone to read. Finally, the women said the letters were making it hard for them because now they knew what the men thought about them. The sharing of the letters was stopped, and no one read the letters except Dad. Besides the letters, the men also sat in a circle confessing sins in front of our boys who knew nothing of married life. This exposed the details of a married couple's bedroom and the whole sex conversation to boys under the age of eighteen What a shame, but my dad said it would be beneficial in the end. Now boys were being put into the coops, too. Elias even put our son Elias Jr. in at age eight. Dad came over and got him out because putting an eight-year-old boy in the coop was uncalled for. At one point, our four oldest boys—Dale, Mark, Eddie, and Dean—were locked up in their rooms confessing sins and writing letters. Absolutely insane. Life was horrible.

Part 4

Separations

– 14 –

Amish Prison

BECAUSE THE MEN THOUGHT THE chicken coop helped straighten up their lives, women were now being sent to the coop. My sister Maggie went first. I will never forget this incident because while she was in there, her husband, Victor, bought hamburgers and grilled them knowing the smell would go to the coop and she would not be able to enjoy the meal. The person in the coop was only allowed bread and water as food—part of the punishment of being in the coop.

Next was Millie, my brother Jonas's wife, who confessed her sins. She used their kids as an excuse to not go to the coop and made Jonas feel guilty because "they needed a mom to care for them." So, Jonas and Millie switched places, and Jonas went into the coop and Millie went to the house. She didn't want to take her punishment, and to me, that was a sign of how manipulative she was. Jonas and Millie were also having marriage issues, so they were hoping their separation would fix their marriage.

Lynn, Leroy Miller's wife, confessed after Millie. Leroy and Lynn admitted they were having marriage issues, too. Lynn stayed in the coop for about three weeks, but because they had kids to care for, Lynn went home during the daytime. After Lynn's three weeks were up, Leroy went to the coop. They agreed that both had been causing their marriage problems.

As we were eating lunch one day, my mom, Susie, came to our house asking for help with changing her life. She had been in the coop and now was being moved from the coop to my upstairs. I was to care for her, making sure she had breakfast and her meals. She was not easy to care for either. One day she would want crackers; the next day cookies. However, I was just supposed to give her bread and water. What a life!

Lies

Elias was back in the coop confessing his sins and writing them down. Nothing he wrote helped him get out, so he started writing lies. As we read what he wrote, it seemed to match his behavior, so we took it as truth. Exactly four weeks to the day that he entered the coop, his brothers Silas and Stephen from Ashland came to visit him. I asked Elias if he wanted to visit with them or wanted them to go home. He sent word to me that they needed to go home and leave him alone. They left, and that night Dad sent word to me that Elias could come out of the coop. When he came out, he shaved, and I gave him a haircut. During his time in the coop, I had made sure Elias had meals. My orders from

Dad were to give him bread and water only, but sometimes I gave him extra food. I knew he was hungry. By this point, I didn't care anymore what Dad said.

When the others found out that writing the lies helped Elias get out of the coop, they started writing lies, too, so they could be freed. One of the lies that Elias wrote was that he had had sex with his mom and that his brother Dan was his child. He told me he thought it was okay to write that because he told himself that it was not true. But the lie matched his actions, and as we always say, "The truth will set you free." We figured that if these letters were setting people free, what they wrote must have been the truth even though they were saying it was lies.

Well, not long after Elias was released, someone caught him in another lie. Elias discovered that someone planned to come after him, so he dressed up with his hat rolled up on both sides, tied a strap around his waist, and left his shoes untied. At dark, he and I walked over to my dad's house. All the men were outside in the shed butchering deer meat. I asked Elias what his plans were, and he said, "Don't worry."

"Listen," I said, "If you plan to throw some words at them, you'd better know what you are talking about, or it will not go well for you."

"Don't worry," he said again.

He went into the shed and tried to get all the men to turn against my dad and to plan an attack on the ones in the house. No one was interested, so he went to the house alone. He went straight for my brother Chester and said, "You know you are not rid of your dirty mind, and you are trying to make it look like you are innocent and working your way up to sit next to Dad." (Within the community, sitting next to my dad meant you had clearly confessed and were forgiven for what you had done in the past.)

Those words made Chester angry. He stood up and started hitting Elias, and Elias hit back. Hitting back was so unlike Elias. My brother Levi stood up, and Elias hit him, too. Now, it was two against one, and they fought until blood was running on the floor and Dad finally said, "Enough!" (This is the same fight where Elias ripped open Chester's pants.)

Chester held Elias down while Levi found a rope. They tied him up around the legs and neck and drug him outside through the main door, hitting his head on the steps as they went out. Later, Chester admitted that he purposely hit Elias's head to try to knock him out, but it didn't work.

Chester and Levi left Elias lying there in the yard while they went back inside to get something. When they went back out, Elias was gone and just the rope was on the ground. Only one thing to do—a search party began. I had to stay inside; they would not let me go out to look for Elias. I begged, but to no avail. The answer was "NO!"

Since I didn't want our kids to know what had happened or where we were, I slept on the couch at my dad's house. Finally, around three o'clock in the morning, the men came into the house with Elias. He was taped with duct tape and his face was black and blue from being beat. Dad said to Elias, "So, it didn't work to lie your way out of the coop after all, did it?"

Elias answered, "No."

My dad then decided to lock up Elias in the barn stalls at my brother Elmer's place. The stalls now became the Amish Prison.

In the meantime, my son Eddie had been locked up in his room writing down his sins and I found a paper where he had drawn a picture of the devil. The picture looked exactly like the way Elias had dressed, and Elias had even remarked that he was the biggest devil on earth. So, I thought Eddie's drawing meant he was just like Elias. I told my dad about the drawing, and the men went and put Eddie in the Amish Prison with Elias. Eddie begged Dad saying that he didn't want to go with his dad, but Dad said, "Ask your dad to let you go free."

Leon Miller, who had been staying at our house while he worked on his anger problem, went to Elmer's house to take care of the prisoners, making sure they had food and water and other needs taken care of.

Somehow Sheriff Frank Abrams found out about people going back to Elmer's house and drove out to check it out. Elias and Eddie had left the barn to go into the house, but before they reached the house, Dad stopped them. Dad knew about the sheriff coming, and he sent Elias and Eddie to the hayloft in his barn so Frank wouldn't see Elias's badly bruised face. It worked; Frank did not find out.

Once Eddie was locked up, my other children found out what was going on. They were terrified because we were hoping we would have a good outcome for our family. Instead, it was worse than ever. Now two of my family members were locked up, and

I was told not to talk to Elias or Eddie. It was a terror for me. My other boys—Dale, Martin, and Dean—were there to help me.

Then Elias escaped, and no one could find him. Someone told me that my brother Chester slept with a knife under his pillow the night Elias escaped. I was upset and furious because I had been told that there would be no weapons involved, just arguing and verbal fighting. Eventually, Elias, who had been sleeping in the schoolhouse, decided to walk home. The men were waiting for him, and he walked right to them. They captured him and taped him up.

Every evening, Elias and Eddie were brought to my dad's house because everyone else was there. The first night Elias and Eddie came up to Dad's house they had twine around their necks because of bad behavior. Dad wanted to show the community what happens if you try to walk over him. After a while, Dad let Eddie come home. Eddie had refused to talk to his own dad while in the Amish Prison.

— 15 —

Haircuts

THINGS STARTED CHANGING FAST. NOW the ones running the show were Chester, Leroy, Randel, and Joseph Mast. The rest knew nothing about what was going on with the men. The women—Mindy Miller, my sister Winnie, and myself—took over the women's problems. I cared for my own family plus had the responsibility of the church. To give myself time to take care of the church issues, I taught my kids to do housework. They did a good job, too. Think about how things were in our Amish community; I taught my boys to do laundry, cook, bake, and clean. They could do the chores as well as any girl could. I often said I could put my boys up against any girls and the boys would win the competition.

One day, Dad said more hair needed to be cut to put fear in the men to not do what Elias had done. He knew that if he cut the men's hair, they wouldn't dare talk back to him or attack him. Dad acted as though he feared all the men left in Bergholz because of Elias's actions. (To this day, I still believe my dad was scared.) Dad also made everyone believe he was a "man after God's own heart." Saying those words showed the men that they needed to respect my dad because they wouldn't go against God. It was so wrong for my dad to say that.

First, Chester and Joseph Mast took Forrest Burkholder and surprised him with scissors and shavers. They shaved him bald. Forrest was told to write a letter about how this made him feel so my dad would know his thoughts.

Ed Miller was brought out of the coop next. They took him to Dad's house so the men could give him a shave and a haircut. Wow! He looked completely different! He was a changed man—very handsome—and all the women talked about it and told Louisa that she had a very handsome man. I know he caught my attention, but I kept it to myself. Somehow this man made me feel different about life. Who knows why? I was very moved and felt respected when he was around. At the time, I didn't know why he made me feel special, but in later years, I discovered why Ed was special in my life, and I will reveal those details in another book.

The rest of the men were given haircuts, too. Somehow my sons Dale and Eddie were the only boys who received a haircut. Bad or good? I didn't know. I was numb; my body and my mind hurt. I didn't know anymore who I was or how to feel. Elias and I had always been close, or so I thought, so being apart and watching things be done to my family was very tough for me.

The men all had different hairstyles given by my brother Levi and Joseph Mast. Dale had a perfect cross on the top of his head; Mervin Miller had a fence around his head; and Leroy Miller had rows, like hay rows, around his head. Besides getting their hair cut, each one was told to sit in the middle of the room and answer questions. If they were caught in a lie, they were smacked on their head with a raw egg. If they fought hard, everyone pitched in to calm them down. They had no choice but to obey and follow the rules whether they agreed or not.

Then Dad told the ladies to walk up to the men and offer them a piece of candy to see what their reaction was. Most of the men ignored the ladies, but Ed Miller grabbed my brother Jonah's wife Millie, put her on his lap, and kissed her! He was a fighter no matter who said what; he was Ed Miller and his actions showed very clearly. In other words, he was not bluffed, so we decided that Millie was way out of place to do such a thing even if she was told to do it. She had the right to refuse. What woman would walk up to another man like that? And Jonas was there, too. Millie also did the same thing to my brother Delbert.

Dad told Louisa to sit on his lap, and she did. Then Dad said to Ed, Louisa's husband, "This is how you hold a woman. Don't grab her and kiss her like you did Millie." Dad was trying to make Ed look bad in front of Louisa. He was standing between Ed and Louisa for a reason that will be revealed later.

Women's Hair Cutting

One day during our visit, Elias mentioned cutting a woman's

hair. He said he knew that some women had the same problem that he had. If we cut his hair, we should also cut some women's hair. My sister Maggie was having problems, so she was the first to get her hair cut and then thrown into the same Amish Prison as the men.

Next, it was Millie followed by my mom. Mom just sat there until Dad said, "Shall I start a fire? Mom, are you just going to sit there and let them cut your hair? You know you don't have to." Mom started to resist and did she ever fight! Mindy Miller was hurt—I guess Mom bit her hand pretty bad, but alas, Mom's hair was cut. We would all take turns cutting off some hair until all women had a turn.

Now, there were three men and three women living in the same house, which was not good. Elias had a bad habit of using other women to try to make me jealous of him and it usually worked; manipulation of the brain is no good. He knew my every mood and mood swing and pushed the right button at the right time. Because Elias always wanted me to feel bad that he was with another woman, the situation at the Amish Prison worked in his favor. He had the upper hand. It would take something stronger than I to overcome the feeling of jealousy.

In the meantime, those of us not in the Amish Prison went on with normal life—cooking, washing dishes, doing laundry, and going to school. We also had Ladies' Day every Wednesday at Mom's house. We would help Mom, when she wasn't in the prison, if there was something to do. If not, we would bring something along to do for ourselves. So, we lived our lives.

Separations

My son Eddie was with Elias for almost a month while the rest of us were at our house. It was tough, but I thought I could handle it. It was winter, so the leaves were off the trees, and I could see back to the house where Elias and Eddie were 24/7. That was very hard.

Anyway, all of us would go to my dad's house every night. The ones sitting on the couch always talked to the others to get them to repent from their sinful life. They would not. We women would talk to the ladies to get them to repent, but that didn't work either.

During the day, all the ones living in Elmer's house went to Dad's house to help with the work. One night my sister Lucille told me that Lynn and Millie were helping in the wash house cleaning up and were making fun of the rest of us that were not there. Then Lucille told me that Elias and Millie had been flirting all day! When they were eating dinner, they would sit and watch each other like a husband and wife and would keep smiling at each other. I knew Elias had that problem anyway, but I was upset and decided to take Millie and Lynn plus all their things and make them stay at my sister Maggie's house. I needed to get them away from the men. My dad had butchered a whole beef which meant the women would have plenty to do. We loaded up all that meat and sent Millie and Lynn away with it. Mom stayed to take care of the men. Every day, we went up to Maggie's house to see how things were going. The women continued getting into huge fights again and again. We tried to deal with it the best we could.

All the couples were now separated except the Able Millers and the Mervin Millers. Louisa, Ed Miller's wife, was now living at my dad's house with her baby girl Betzy who was six weeks old.

Ed was taking care of the rest of the children at his house alone plus going to work during the day. While he was at work, the kids went to Mervin and Em's house so they wouldn't be alone.

Finally, the day came that Mindy Miller, Winnie, and I went around to all the houses to make sure all was being taken care of. Ed was at home that day, sitting in his rocking chair reading a book. The house was not very clean. I was moved and uncomfortable there without realizing what was going on yet. I knew I was drawn to him for some odd reason. I'd never had a problem with other men other than having a hard time forgetting William, my first love. It was very uncommon for me to feel this way in Ed's presence because he was my cousin, and of course, I never told anyone.

We did, however, go home and tell Dad how Ed's house looked. Dad decided that Mom could take her things and move to Ed's house to help. Now the men in the Amish Prison were on their own again, so I felt better. I was furious with my dad that he had put men and women in the same house together, even if it was meant as a "jail" or "prison." People of the world would not do such a thing! We were supposedly godly people and never allowed men and women who were not married to each other to stay in the same house without a spouse present. Dad did anyway. It was so wrong.

– 16 –

More Separation

ON A COLD DAY IN January 2010, it was decided that all couples should separate so that our community could move on. We thought we had to separate everyone before healing and getting back together could start. So, we hitched up the big hay wagon and work horses and drove to Able Miller's and Mervin Miller's houses. We gathered the women and children and drove them to my sister Maggie's house and dropped them off. It was so cold that we worried for a while that some of the kids would freeze in the wagon, but everyone was okay. Amelia, Able Miller's wife, was angry that we took her to Maggie's house because she wanted to be at my dad's house while she was away from her husband. We knew that's what Amelia wanted, and whatever someone "wanted" in life, we made sure that they didn't get it. They got the opposite.

Not long after the women moved to Maggie's house, they got into a huge fight. Maggie took over somehow; I guess she thought that since she had to care for all these women by herself, she got to be the boss. (Her husband Victor was not home at the time because he was spending time in the Amish Prison.) A couple of days later, we went up to see how things were going. Lynn was locked upstairs and not allowed to come down. The story was that the women started arguing about how Lynn thought she was perfect and was acting like she was Jesus, so Amelia squirted ketchup all over Lynn to make it look like blood was pouring from her face. Then Amelia stood back and laughed and laughed at Lynn. We couldn't believe what we had just heard. This was terrible! We brought Lynn downstairs and listened to her side of the story, which matched what the others had said. So, Maggie and the rest received a spanking from us. We took Maggie out to the entrance so the kids wouldn't see what was happening.

Another evening they had prepared their supper—ice cream and pizza—but we "boss" women took their supper to Dad's house and ate it along with the men who were staying in the Amish Prison at the time. The women then had to make soup for their supper. This was another form of punishment for the women for fighting with each other.

I would see Elias almost every night, but I was not allowed to talk to him. In my mind, I loved him more than anything else in the world. Our life was not good, but I was determined to keep us together. The harder I tried, the harder my dad kept pulling us apart. I could depend on Elias having to leave every two to three months and going to live with someone else so he could straighten up his life. The only "charge" that ever came up against him was that he didn't take care of the kids the way my dad thought he should. So, Dad's punishment for Elias was to separate us. Many times, I cried to Dad to let us stay together. Life was so hard alone with no husband to help, but Dad kept telling me it was for Elias's good. Elias also insisted it was okay because he wasn't living the life he should. So, I kept going. I pushed to get things done in the community because I had this idea that the faster we moved forward, the sooner Elias and I could get back together and live our married life the best we could. I also realized that Elias wanted to go live in other places, and it seemed like he was purposely doing things he knew my dad would disapprove of so he could leave me and go live somewhere else. It made me weak because I couldn't fight for someone who didn't want to get help for a better life.

The next time we went up to Maggie's, she, again, was being mean to the ladies. She was thinking the same as I was: the sooner we can get this done, the sooner we can get back together. In her mind, her married life was also not so bad, but she couldn't tell Dad. He had his role to play and was going to do it no matter what anyone else said. Maggie's punishment that day was Winnie taking a wooden spoon and hitting her on top of her head until her eyes were swollen shut and her face was all black and blue. I finally told Winnie to quit beating her. Mindy and I cut Amelia and Lynn's hair down as short as we could and told them to be nice to each other and treat each other like they wanted to be treated. Then we decided to take Millie and Lynn along with Mom back to the Amish Prison with the men.

Now that all married couples had been separated, we were

ready to start healing and getting back together. The separated couples were allowed visitation on Sundays and sometimes during the week. It was time to move on.

Eddie started coming along just fine once he got it in his head that he could not leave the prison and go home whenever he wanted to. He must wait on permission from Dad. At this point, I had all the kids with me except for Eddie. Dale pitched in and helped me more than ever before. Dad said that the only reason Dale was jumping in and helping was because he was afraid that if he didn't, he would have to go to Amish Prison. I didn't believe that, but I could not tell my dad any different. Just so you know, once my dad decided he was going to do something or something was going to be done a certain way, you might as well shut your yap and obey his rules because he would not accept anyone else's opinion or advice. You might state your opinion, but in the end, what he said went unless it worked in his favor or was something he WANTED to do for himself.

I mentioned earlier that my sister Maggie and I could never agree on anything. My mom had fueled that fire, plus our problem was starting to show up in our children's relationships with each other. Because Maggie didn't have as many children as I did, she had more one-on-one time with each of her children than I did with mine. Her children had more expensive things than mine did, so there was friction and jealousy between the families. And when there is friction, you no longer understand each other. That is not good! Long story short, Maggie and I argued a lot.

Mark, my second son, began having problems with feeling

Separations

disowned by everyone. No matter what he did, somehow it was not right. Mark and I had lots of "talks" about life. I knew how he felt, but he didn't believe I did. Not only were there disagreements between Mark and me, but he had problems with his dad as well. Then my dad sent word to my house that Mark needed to pack up and change places with Eddie in Amish Prison. Eddie could come home, but Mark had to go to prison to change his life. As he left the house, I said to him, "Good riddance!" which was not nice of me as a mom, but I was so tired of arguing with him plus he knew exactly what to say to make me cry. So, the exchange was made, and Eddie came home. Even though Mark and I argued, I missed him so much every day after he left. And I wished I hadn't said what I did when he left. I felt so bad about my words. After this, I became weaker and weaker.

About two weeks later, my dad sent word that Dale needed to pack up and leave for the Amish Prison. I was upset but could not disagree with Dad; it wouldn't do me any good. Dale left, and I started getting weaker. With my husband and two oldest sons no longer at home, life was tough. I did my best to brave up and be strong for my kids that were still with me. Eddie had to take all responsibility for our future as the head of the farm and as a father figure while I battled huge feelings of loneliness and insecurity. Although I knew that Elias was not a God-chosen man, I still felt secure when he was there. Now I felt everything was all on me. I could feel my life going down faster and faster; my strength and all I ever believed in started mocking me to my face, but I kept going the best I could. The worst part was getting everyone ready for bed and then waking up alone the next morning. When we went to my dad's house in the evenings, I had to get everyone ready to go and then gather them all up to go back home. Oh my! What a hectic life!

I was told that Dale was begging to come home and was thinking of every excuse he could to be released, but the answer was always NO! Dad had beehives, so Dale took care of Dad's bees plus ours. The rest of the ones living in prison had to work for my dad. They had to do things he never did himself, like fixing his machinery, working in the fields, and cutting wood. The Miller boys were living in their section of Bergholz keeping up the work that needed to be done there while Louisa was at my dad's house and the other Miller ladies were at their homes. (Remember this—there is a reason Dad moved Louisa into his house.)

Life continued as usual. The kids went to school, and I cooked and baked and cleaned the best I could. On Wednesdays, we still went to my mom's for our weekly gathering. Of course, our conversation always went to the Amish Prison people and if anything would change. It seemed like the prisoners could get mad and tell everyone how they felt or they could sit there and cry. A pitiful story. The prisoners were held captive in my dad's power and were not released until he thought they had changed how he wanted them.

Lawsuit

Around the same time my boys were in prison, we were also

Separations

being interviewed because Dad had filed a lawsuit against Sheriff Frank Abrams for putting our school kids through the scare of a SWAT team. Back when my sister Winnie and her husband Adam were having problems, a SWAT team with guns drawn had surrounded the schoolhouse where Winnie was teaching. The kids were terrified and hid under desks and wherever they thought they would be safe. When Winnie went to the door to talk to the sheriff, he said they were there to get Adam's girls because Adam wanted to see them. (My dad had refused to allow Adam to visit at all.) That day was followed by court hearings and a trial to determine full custody of the girls. Now we were back in court because of Dad's lawsuit against Frank. It was stressful gathering in the courtroom knowing that all the men and women were not living together at that time. It was actually embarrassing to meet your own husband in court; one crazy life to live! In the evenings after court, we all gathered at Dad's house to go over all that was said and done.

During court, we found out that Adam had been sitting in the basement of Frank Abrams's office helping plan where the SWAT team with the guns would stand around the schoolhouse and on my dad's property. Their mission had been to get the girls away from Winnie and to hopefully capture Winnie and get the hell away from my dad, but it didn't work out. They got the girls, but not Winnie that day.

Dad won the lawsuit against the sheriff, and all the kids who were involved received a check from the court according to the damage each child went through mentally. My dad and my brother Jonas were angry that the kids received checks. They thought that filing a lawsuit would somehow get Winnie's girls back, but nope, not at all. (Adam had been awarded custody and the girls weren't coming back.) Dad and Jonas asked everyone to agree to rip up their checks and throw them away and that's what was done. The court found out what happened, and they put the children's checks in a savings account for them to pick up once they were eighteen years old.

— 17 —

Visions

My life continued to go downhill. One day my dad hired tree trimmers to come to the farm to trim trees in the front yard. All I could see was that he was making crosses to kill all of us and hang us on tree crosses just like Jesus's own people did to Him. I was so afraid of death. I would yell out, "Somebody help me, so I don't have to die!" But nobody helped me. Instead, they laughed at me for saying such awful things, but to me, my visions were very real.

A truck came driving in the driveway exactly on time . . . the same time that I had heard a train whistle blow to tell me the time was up. I thought the truck driver was going to tie a rope around my stomach and drag me down the road until I was in pieces. After me, it would be the others' turn. I was beside myself yelling for help, but nobody helped me. The truck driver finished what he'd come for and left. I was still on the couch shaking and sweaty, telling the others to make sure their lives were in place because one day we would get killed and it would be OVER FOREVER! If our life is not right, it is too late—but nobody paid attention to me.

The Bergholz people always sat in a circle to visit. The circle was a sign to keep the devil from entering the middle, but in my mind, they were keeping God outside. I walked over to the circle one day, but they had all the chairs tight together so I could not enter. I said to them, "I see that I must walk alone. Like walking to a desert that has no food or water. I don't know if I will make it, but I will take the challenge to try."

I told my dad that I give up, and his answer was "Yeah, I know. Renold says the same thing. I can no longer travel with the Bergholz people."

Meeting

I asked my son Eddie to go to the Amish Prison, get Elias, and bring him to me. I wanted to talk to him. Talking wasn't allowed because we were separated at that time. But the rules didn't matter to me anymore. I had convinced myself that I was the person who had done wrong and that I needed to make this clear to everyone.

As Elias came toward me, I walked to him and told him that I never stood with my dad, I did not believe like he did, and I was pretending all along. Elias said that it was too late for those things. I told him that what I meant was that I disagreed with helping ban Lawrence Troyer and his family, and since they had already left the community, it didn't matter anymore if I'd agreed or not. The fight was over. The reason I mentioned Lawrence was because my dad had made the church rule that whoever agrees with that family would get the same punishment they had: six months ban. So, I thought I was like Lawrence's family and took the punishment. Nobody, not even me, could understand what was happening in my life right then because I had always been on my dad's side strong and hard.

Just then, the other men saw me talking to Elias and knew we were not supposed to. They stepped between us and made him leave. They told Elias that even if I sent for him, he knew he was to stay away. He should have refused to talk to me, but he knew I was weak, and of course, he was happy to talk to me. It was like he knew that I would take the blame for him and he let me do it, although he clearly knew that I was not the problem in our family.

In looking back, I had to take the blame so that I could free myself from all the sin going on behind the scenes that I was not aware of. God knew! I was so scared and shaken that I cried out to God with all my heart and soul to stop whatever was happening to my life and to please spare me from the devil's grip. I had felt the evil spirit grabbing me by my throat and trying to choke me. He held a knife to my face and said, "Repent or I will kill you." I was scared out of my mind! My mind said to me, "Your blood would taste so good right now." Then I heard the sharpening of knife blades, and when I looked around, I saw knives hanging on the wall. I screamed out in real life so loud that my children were scared.

The knives I'd seen were actually hanging there on the wall. Elias and my sons used them along with guns for hunting deer. I knew my vision with the knives represented my life and I knew that I was going to get killed. My life was going downhill fast and ending soon. The worst of it would happen in April 2010.

Part 5

Rejection

– 18 –

More Visions

MY MIND KEPT TELLING ME that everything was just a fool's story; it was not happening in real life. Yet I also knew and felt that it was real. In looking back, I know that I was not in my right mind for about a month, but I was talking like I knew what I was saying. While my life was such a mess, God let me see the future on so many things that blew my mind.

My daughter Eve wanted us to stay at my dad's house for the night because she was scared, so we did. Ed and the boys slept in the upstairs of my dad's shop, and the little ones and I slept on the living room floor. Well, that was not a good idea because the things that had happened and were said when my brother Elmer was possessed kept going through my mind. I felt that everything was my fault. While I was lying on the floor unable to sleep, I saw lots of chapters of my life going through my mind.

Earlier, I had told Elias that it looked like he and I had to go our separate ways because we are so different. Since we had ten children, he would get five, and I would get five so that neither of us would be too lonely while we were separated. Well, that night, some of the other families had left children at my dad's house to sleep on the floor, too. During the night, adults were walking back and forth taking children away. When I woke up, all I could see was that Elias had taken our oldest five and left me with the five youngest to care for. I had no idea how I would care for them, and it was driving me insane! Then I actually woke up. Everyone was still there! Thank you, God! (The events from my dream would take place in reality several years later. The only difference was the five oldest were not living with Elias, but on their own, because of situations in the community. The only ones who continued to live with him were Eddie and Eve because they stayed with the Amish and the rest of us did not. Eve promised me that if things did not work out with Dad she would come and live with me. So, I already knew that separation from some of my children would happen sooner or later in life. The only reason my dad allows Eve to stay in the community is for revenge on me; she was the only tool he had left. He never liked Elias and would not start liking him now.) I told my brother all that I had seen and heard in the night, and I told him Elias was the one who would kill me. My brother said that he knew I would probably tell him that.

The next night I was chilled through and through and sitting in the rocking chair with a blanket. I had not slept or eaten anything for two days now. My mouth was very dry, so I asked my dad

Rejection

for a Mountain Dew. He told me that the Bible says we need to feed the poor, and then he let me have one.

That night the children started singing the song about "I never saw my dad in the church of God." And I said, "Dad, do you hear what they are singing?"

"Yes," he said. "That means all the dads of this church are guilty of not being a true dad to their children. They have never been seen in the church of God!"

But no, the kids were singing it to my dad. I was the one down and struggling about all the things my dad was doing and I knew the song was directed at him. The other men from the church were not my dad. My dad was the one separating the dads and moms with children together and who were married for a reason that God allowed to happen. My dad was responsible for his actions. Nobody else. He argued that a lot. Also, Dad kept saying that Adam Troyer, my brother-in-law, would be going to prison for the rest of his life for what he did to my sister Winnie. When I was out of my usual mind, I told Dad that he is the Adam Troyer he kept talking about and he would be sentenced to life in prison. Of course, he denied what I said. He said it would never happen. (But later in life, it did.)

Another thing God showed me was that while I was protecting Elias from my dad all those years, Elias was cheating on me, and therefore, it was now time for me to leave my family and move on. God allowed this to happen. Elias would now stay with my dad, but I could not. I thought God was very cruel to let this happen to me. There was no way on earth that I could just walk away and leave the man I had protected all those years. But I could no longer live in the home we had built, and I needed to leave. I screamed many times, which made my children afraid of me. I had no clue what was going to happen next. I was so scared. In my mind, I was thinking about the future and what will happen years later.

After staying at my dad's house, they made me go home to my house and care for my children. At this point, Dale and Mark were still in the Amish Prison. Elias was living at Able Miller's house as his punishment for talking to me, plus I was afraid of him because I knew he had cheated on me and had another woman's heart. I became angry at Dad because I knew if he had not separated us, none of this would have happened. But I could not change it; what's done is done.

I stayed at my house for three days. I begged Dad to let me take my things and move to the shop upstairs and just live there. My house was no longer my home and I felt out of place. I kept saying that the Ed Millers were taking my house away because my dad took their house and they had no place to go. If I didn't stay there, it might come true, but I did not have any energy left to stay. So, I took what things we needed and moved the children to the upstairs above the shop at my dad's place until I could figure out what I was supposed to do.

We did the best we could, but now life was even harder than it should have been. The boys had to walk over every morning to do the chores. We had horses, chickens, rabbits, ducks, turkeys, dogs, and cats to feed and care for. Every now and then my boys would come up to the shop and beg me to go home because they did not

Rejection

believe their dad would harm me. I was accused of being out of my mind, but by now everything had settled down enough that I knew that it was the real true God who had showed me the future for our life. Every time I went home, a car drove in the driveway and my mind told me it was Elias spying on me. I was afraid that, if I did go home to stay and Elias found out, he wouldn't kill me but would send someone else to do it. So, I refused.

Before I go much farther . . . I had been praying and asking God why our marriage seemed to be ruined and why it was not what I wanted in life. God told me that he would show me why our marriage was ruined. He also warned me that nobody would believe me when he showed me about Elias and the woman he cheated on me with because it was my sister-in-law, my brother Jonas's wife, Millie. I asked God, "Well, how will I know what you showed me is true?" His answer was "Listen to the remarks that will come from Millie and Elias, and they will tell you it is true. Watch their actions. I will allow things to happen in front of you so you can see."

Because I felt like I didn't belong at my dad's house, I no longer went there with everyone else. However, I would watch out my window when all the rest of them were there and getting ready to leave to go home. It was dark outside one evening when I saw Elias standing in front of my mom's bulk food store and looking toward my window. Millie came out of the house, walked up to Elias, and handed him her baby. Elias held the baby for a while before handing her back to Millie. He took the baby and held it for a bit. I know both Elias and Millie knew I was watching. As this happened, I felt all the ties between Elias and me being cut off. We were no longer as one. He divorced me when he cheated, and I could feel it. I felt as dead as a stone, like all the blood had drained from my body. I couldn't fall asleep that night until past three. When I finally fell asleep, I had a vision dream.

Elias had his church suit on and walked toward me. I asked him, "When did this happen, Elias, that you have a baby with Millie?"

He answered, "We did it on Sunday evenings when we were at your dad's house. Upstairs." When we went visiting at my dad's house on Sundays, Elias always held one of our little ones until they fell asleep. Then he would carry them upstairs to sleep. Millie also had children and took them upstairs when they fell asleep. I saw Elias and Millie do this many times, but not once did it occur to me that they would be doing such things as having sex upstairs before they came back down. I trusted them. I shouldn't have. The vision in my dream was the first answer from God.

The next day I saw death on all my children's faces because Elias had cut the bloodline between his very own flesh and blood for another woman who was another man's wife. He killed our own children spiritually, plus me. Just as I had been told—he was going to kill me, and it happened in a way nobody believed. I was the only one that could see and feel death among us just like God told me. All the rest of them mocked me and scorned me. I was thrown out of Dad's house for talking about things that were true and real. I was disowned, rejected by my own family. They took Elias's side because he told them that he did not divorce me or kill us. He knew what he had done, and Millie did, too. In the spiritual life, we were dead.

Well, the time came that my brother Chester and his family needed a different house to live in, so Dad said I needed to leave the upstairs above the shop. The men from the prison would live in the upstairs, and Chester would move into the house where the prison had been. Chester had planned to fix up an old trailer sitting beside the road, so I told my dad to bring that old trailer down to his farm and put it back by the pigpen for me to live in for a while. I was too scared to go home.

The children and I moved into the trailer, and it was a nasty one to live in. Nobody helped me clean it up or fix it. The trailer was not leveled at all. When it rained, it rained inside because the door would not close properly. Our mattress was on the floor with no frame, and it got wet from the rain. I used water from the lake right beside us for taking baths and washing dishes. We had a jug to get drinking water from my dad. We ate cornflakes and white crackers and milk. I gave my dad a list of groceries, and he got what I wrote down without asking questions. I tell you, nobody came to offer help or see if we needed anything. We lived a very dirty, nasty life because I knew we were dead and who wants to care for dead people?

I did not want to live anymore and begged God to just take me and my kids away, but he said, "No, I have something else for you." The pain was almost unbearable, yet I lived day by day and my soul was in hot hell being burned and tortured 24/7. If anyone wonders what hell is like, I can explain: it melts the skin off your body but does not burn your body to ashes. It continues to torture you like that—hot beyond anything I can think of. On top of that, your mind works like a broken record: whatever happened in your life that made you miserable goes through your mind 24/7. It's the only thing playing in your mind and nothing else, and you cannot get away from it because you are captured in your own life. What continuously went through my mind was that my husband, Elias, cheated on me with my brother's wife, Millie, and Elias had children with her. The children were alive and walking in front of me, but nobody could see who they really were except for me.

Finally, I started getting a little bit better. I occasionally walked over to my dad's house, went inside, and sat on a chair to see if they would accept me now. Slowly, but surely, they did as long as I kept my mouth shut about Elias and Millie. Just think, knowing what I did and knowing that Elias and Millie knew, but we couldn't talk about it. I tried my best to keep quiet and talk about other things. I even explained to Dad how the trailer was not level and our mattress got wet when it rained, so he sent Victor and Leon back to work on it. They were men who were living in prison—outcasts.

While I had been living upstairs in Dad's shop, something told me that Elias had taken my name off our checking account. I tried my best to tell Dad about this. Every time my dad went out to the barn to do chores, I would walk behind him telling him that Elias was going to marry another woman: Millie, my sister-in-law. I had no home to live in with my children and Elias had already taken my name off the checking account. I also told Dad that Elias was going to take my house away from me and kick me and the children out.

Dad would yell at me and say, "Stop saying such stupid things! You know Elias would never do such a thing!"

I begged my dad to listen to me. I told him, "I am telling you the truth!" (Later in the second book about my life, you will see that what I tried to tell Dad actually happened. I *was* telling him the truth.)

I had no idea what was happening in my life. I knew something terrible was going on, but I didn't know what. My family thought I was crazy and jealous. This happened in April 2010. Later in June, when I went home, I had to go to the bank to put my name on our checking account. Elias *had* taken my name off. He had kept the old checkbook to show them that my name was still on the account. It was a lie! Not my truth.

— 19 —

Leaving

Alexander, Ivan, and Jeremy were living with Elias up at the Miller section of Bergholz. They lived in a trailer that they did not need either at the time. Eve, Ervin, and Stephen were with me in my trailer. Dale, Mark, Eddie, and Dean stayed in the shop with the men. Stephen would beg to visit his dad, but my dad refused to let him or the others visit Elias for whatever reason. I did not blame them for wanting to see their dad since I was not being a very nice mom at the time. Elias was still their dad, and he would have cared for them if they visited with him. But my dad always said NO to visiting.

The growing season was starting, and someone needed to plant the crops at our farm. Dad told Elias he could come back if I didn't want to do the work. Dad also told Elias that if he went home, I would go home, too. But I didn't know that was said. I had no plans to go home. My family thought I was crazy in my head

Rejection

because I could not be with Elias and because I wanted sex and could not have it. They thought that, if they put us back together, I would be fine, but that was not the case at all. I felt lonely with nobody to talk to and to share my feelings with about what I was told by God. Anyway, Elias moved back to our house, and my dad assumed I was leaving, too, but I did not trust Elias enough just then to live with him.

Late one Saturday evening around midnight, I was in bed sleeping when something pushed my bed and woke me up. A voice told me to go to the kitchen and look out the window, so I did. The moon was shining brightly, and I spotted Elias walking up my dad's driveway toward my trailer. However, when he reached the barn, he turned and went up the hill toward the hayloft on my brother Jonas's property. Just as he was about to enter, I saw Millie walking from her house. She walked up the hill toward the hayloft as well, and together they entered the hayloft. I was beside myself, but I remembered what God had told me: "I will make things happen so you can see that it is true." I went back to bed but did not sleep until early morning. I was angry at Elias and Millie and also at God for allowing this to happen and then showing me in real life that it was true. God knew that I could not talk to anyone about this.

The next day was Sunday and everyone gathered at my dad's house as usual, everyone but me. I waited until I knew that everyone was there. I gathered some crackers and water and a coat and had plans to leave for forever—never return. I walked all the way back to the big hill, climbed it, and kept walking into the woods as far as I could until there was no more path to follow. After about two hours of walking, I stopped and let my mind rest and thought about whether I really wanted to do this.

I knew that if anyone realized I was gone, there would be an alarm going off. I started to think about my children. Little Jeremy was about three years old. It was not his fault or any of their faults that my marriage to Elias was ruined. I also knew that as their mom it was not right for me to leave them. I had a hard time liking my children at this point, but I guess I still had some feelings left. I sat there for a while to decide what I wanted to do. I finally decided to head home.

As I was walking through the pasture, I stopped and laid down flat on my back. I looked at the sky and wondered if God knew where I was and why was He doing this to me. Then I prayed and asked Him to forgive me for all my wrongdoings. I asked Him to give me another chance so I could prove to Him I could somehow handle this situation. When I finished praying, I walked home to the trailer.

Nobody knew the battle I was in between good and evil. I loved my children so much that I did not want them to grow up and find out what their dad had done. I had a terrible time fighting against that and was battling suicidal thoughts. I tried to think of how I could end my life without suspicion or without it being my fault, but I found no way. I even tried to think of ways to commit suicide with my children, too. I was in a battle that I cannot explain. I tried to drown my baby in a mud puddle. But I couldn't. I thought of setting the trailer on fire during the night while my children slept in it, but I couldn't do that either. I loved my children too much. None of what happened was the children's fault.

Not long after I almost left, I was cooking for the men who lived in the shop. On this particular day, my dad told all the kids to go home and help Elias clean up the farm since nobody had lived there for two months. The farm was dirty, the grass needed to be cut, the garden needed attention—I didn't even know that the boys had planted a garden. That evening, Dale, who was working a job, was not on the truck with the other workers. All the kids were at home with Elias, and I assumed Dale was too. My mind did a flip-flop. Everyone was home now except Mom. As I thought about this, I looked out the window and spotted Millie, with her baby in a wagon, walking across the field toward my house. My next thought drove me crazy: "If she gets there before me, I will lose everything that I have—my home, my kids, plus my man!"

I stepped away from the window, put on my shoes, and started running across the field. I couldn't see Millie anymore, but I kept running until I got to our driveway. I stayed on my side of the road because in my mind our house was no longer my home. Mark, who was working in the garden, saw me and came over to ask what was going on. He went to get Elias so I could talk to him and ask him how he was. Now, remember, this would be the first time I'd see Elias's face to face since I knew the truth about him, so I was very shaken.

I asked Elias if Millie was there and he said no. I have no clue what happened to her or where she went, but I beat her to my house. Then I asked Elias if he would care if I came home to start our life over. He said that since I had opened my arms for him when he was in the chicken coop and gave him more food than I was supposed to, it was his turn to open his arms. He invited me back home, and on July 22, 2010, I moved home with all our stuff, and I abandoned the trailer. When I had seen Millie walking over toward my house, it had been a spiritual vision that disappeared but, to me, was very real.

Our house looked so beautiful after living above the shop and in a rundown trailer for months. I cannot describe the beauty, yet I had a guilty feeling that made me feel horrible. I kept thinking, "I stole my farm back. I am sleeping with somebody else's man." A very weird feeling. Things returned to usual with me and the six youngest kids at home. The four oldest did not trust me nor Elias anymore. Poor kids. I felt so bad about all that happened!

God spoke to me again after I moved home and said, "Because you now choose to go back when I told you this place is no longer yours, when the time is right, your boys will leave this community and go to live in the world and choose a life of their own."

I lost it again and told Elias. Of course, he didn't believe me, but he said, "Always remember: if we lose the older four boys, we still have five more coming up to help us pay the bills and raise the rest of the family." I didn't like his advice, but it calmed me down. I tried to forget what God told me. I tried to convince my mind that God lied to me and those things would not happen. Deep inside, I wished I would have stayed away, but it was too late.

I had a bad habit of talking to myself out loud because I had nobody to talk to who would believe me. When I moved back home with Elias, I quit talking to myself. To my family, it looked like they were right—all I needed was Elias. But what they didn't know was Elias slapped me across my face and told me to stop talking to myself NOW! After that, I never talked to myself whenever I thought he or anyone else would see me. I did not care if my family thought they were right, and I did not try to explain. I was still in my own life's cage as a prisoner.

As time went on the boys started to move home. Dale came home first and soon after Dean followed. But Eddie and Mark stayed at the shop. I would talk to them occasionally, but not often.

— 20 —

Trouble

SOON AFTER I MOVED HOME, someone else always lived in our house with us. Dad moved these people into our house, and we were never alone as a family. We had Ed Miller with five of his kids and all their belongings, my mom, my sister Maggie, and Millie and all her things. (Our house was so full we had to put Millie's stuff on our back porch.) We also had Leon and all his things, and Valerie and her kids plus some of their things. And all of my mom's things!

I told Chester to come and get his family and take them home and care for them as a family, but he said, "Dad told me to bring Valerie here, and I will listen to him first." I told him I would not listen to Dad because all he was doing was tearing families apart and it was not good. My sister Abigail came to stay for a day or two, and she told Valerie to go home, but Valerie was too scared. Later, my son Eddie told me that my dad put all these people in my house hoping that I could not handle the turmoil and would come live in his house. I was so angry at Dad that it was not funny.

For years, my mom had a bulk food store. One day the girls moved my mom off my dad's farm for good. They gathered all her belongings in the house and everything from the store. They loaded all of it in a big hay wagon and dumped it in a huge pile in our yard. There were lots of bulk items the girls did not want any longer, plus rolls and rolls of material. All piled in our yard. Some of it got very dirty. They even made her change her address to ours. Why did they do this? Because my dad had decided to kick Mom out of her own house and move Louisa and all her things in. Dad was replacing Mom with Louisa, another man's wife. I sent word to my dad that our house was full enough and there was no more room for anybody else.

If you remember, my mom and I did not always get along very well. Things were a mess until we figured out where to store everything until she found a place to sell it. Elias told her she had a week to get rid of everything or else he would load it all up and take it to the Rogers Machinery sale. Mom cried so much. She and Elias argued about this until finally she got her way and made him give her more time. While everything with mom was happening, the kids got into fights time and again that needed settled, plus the adults started arguing among themselves. What a life!

To add more to my struggles, Millie was pregnant, and of course, I believed it to be Elias's child. Millie, and Elias too, continued making the remarks that God had told me to be aware of. Nobody else heard these remarks like I did because I was the only one to believe what God told me. In the evenings after supper, Millie would take Valerie's baby and rock her and sing "You Are My Sunshine." Elias pretended to be reading the paper, but he would sing with her, even when I was sitting right beside his rocking chair. He knew I could hear them singing. When my life crashed, the same spirit that had talked to me all my life told me that all of Millie's children with blonde hair and blue eyes were Elias's babies. The dark hair and brown-eyed ones were her husband Jonas's children.

In time, I realized that not all the blame I placed on myself for my broken marriage was true because Millie had stepped between us first. After that, I no longer felt guilty and I started to make remarks back to them, I think they realized that what they said and did no longer affected me. I started becoming a lot stronger.

Millie didn't seem to care that I knew she was sleeping with my husband. She kept telling me that she had never stayed home from the hospital to have a baby, but this time she was going to. She said when she did, she would sleep in my bed and I would have to go upstairs to sleep. I told her, "No, that's my bedroom! If you have that baby in my house, you will get a half bed set up in my living room. It's just too bad I have so many people at my house!" I was angry at her by now and didn't care anymore that she knew I was angry. I thought it was disgusting of her to step between a man and his wife and boast about it. She tore our family apart forever. I know that she will pay the consequences once God says, so I trust in my God.

Dad's Trouble

When Dad moved Louisa into his house, we found out that he was in some serious trouble. He had been taking turns sleeping with the other women of the community. He claimed that the women were afraid of their own husbands and wanted to get their strength back to live with their husbands. And in order to get their strength back, they took turns sleeping with my dad. Most of the husbands had admitted that they got themselves into sin and spent some time in the chicken coops to improve their marriages.

It appears, in looking back, that he searched for the right woman to take my mom's place (even though she was still alive). During the day while the men were at work, he made his rounds to all the women's houses to talk to them. To hide his actions, he also stopped at some of his daughters' houses to visit. He told the women that because he was the bishop, they must tell him everything and honor his wishes. So, the women really had no choice if he wanted one of them to live with him or sleep with him. They were to respect his wishes because he was "a man of God." What he did not know or care about was he was using God's name in vain to cover up sins. His actions and the things he talked about were not godly at all. He told me himself that he had lusty thoughts. He tried coming to my house, but I kicked him out whenever I was alone. I only let him in when Elias was home, and I would sit in the living room while Dad and Elias talked. The other ladies could've done the same thing and stand up for themselves, but they didn't.

Remember, I was the one who had told everyone that my dad was a man of God and that if you sat close to him, you could feel strength coming from him. They tried it and it worked for them, but it no longer worked for me because Dad did not believe what I told him and he went against me. He rejected me and cast aside everything I said. He and I were no longer a team. I planned to stay away from Dad as far as I could. I was upset about his choice to kick my mom out of her house. He believed she had cheated on him, but even if she did, he had no right to do the same. Personally, I don't believe Mom cheated.

Dad told me God told him he was going to have another big buggy-load of children, but since Mom was too old, he had a right to choose a younger woman and have more kids. So, he did. We found out that Mindy Miller had been sleeping with Dad, but because she could not get pregnant, she lost her seat beside Dad to Louisa. I was there at my dad's house the evening Louisa and Mindy changed their chairs around. Louisa now sat next to my dad like she was his wife. My mom had to see Louisa sitting next to Dad every time she visited on Sunday evenings and Wednesday evenings.

Soon we heard some bad news: Louisa was gaining weight and looking heavier. She had always been skinny, so we all tried telling ourselves that she was just feeling better. However, when Ed, her husband, went over to visit her one day, she asked him if he noticed she was gaining weight. Ed said he did and asked her why.

"Well," she said, "I am pregnant. I don't want you to cry all over the place. You need to stand up and be a man!"

Rejection

Ed turned as white as a sheet of linen. Things were too much for him. First, he lost his house where he was, and now his wife was taken away from him. He did not want anything like this to happen. He said their marriage was okay until my dad stepped in between them. (Later, I heard Louisa say those exact same words, but it was too late.)

My dad told Louisa the baby would bring the community closer together, but he was wrong, so very wrong! The boys living upstairs above the shop found out what happened, so Dad made Louisa gather all the women in a circle and tell them what happened, and Ed was to do the same with the men. Meanwhile, Dad was in bed flat on his back and not showing his face at all.

Ed was furious. He was now headed down the same road I was on earlier when I found out about Elias. The only difference was Ed had actual proof while my story that I could not talk about was only meant for me to know. When Ed found out Louisa was pregnant, he was living at our house, so I kept an eye on him. I would hear him coming downstairs and walking around like a lost soul. I would hear the door open and close again and again. To me, his face was too white and scared looking. Time after time I would see him sitting in the dark corner and I would tell him not to—"Stay in the light as much as you can." Oh, how I longed to reach out to this man and just protect him from what he had to face. He loved his wife, and now his marriage was ruined. My dad had stepped between them, just like Millie had stepped between Elias and me. I knew exactly what Ed was going to face, feelings and all.

My mom ... Oh, my word. I can't even express what she was

going through, knowing she would have to see my dad and Louisa every time she went over there. She sat and cried to the point that it worked on my nerves. I knew the kids wanted to know why she was crying, but it was too difficult to explain. Because my mom and I had a hard time getting along, Elias said that our house was too full. Since it was summertime, Mom bought a huge tent and Elias told me to move Mom's things out of the house and into her tent. I asked her to move out to the tent because the children were asking a lot of questions, too. So, she was living out there in the tent, and I got blamed for it. But, guess what? I no longer cared what I got blamed for. I knew what was true and what was not, so it did not matter to me anymore. I felt sorry for Mom even though we had problems; she was still my mom.

Birds

One day I took Ed's girls and my Eve to a flea market to have a day away from work. I bought the girls a cockatiel in a cage. Afterward, we stopped at Wendy's to eat and had a good time. Later, I found out that my mom was angry at me because she was supposed to be taking care of Ed's girls, not me.

The cockatiel was a very noisy bird, and his cage hung on the windowsill close to Ed's chair. It seemed like every time we wanted to talk that bird was noisy. Ed would yell at it to shut up. I will never forget that! Before I bought the cockatiel, Dale had purchased a parakeet, and my sister Lucille also had one. Now that we had our bird, everyone else thought they wanted a bird, too.

This is something the community had a bad habit of doing—if one person had something, everyone else wanted that thing. Suddenly, we ended up with all the birds because my family said we were the ones to bring the birds into the community. It was like the birds were a curse or something. I thought the whole situation was very strange, indeed.

Revenge

The horse sale was coming up at the Mount Hope auction. We all wanted to attend, but we knew we couldn't all go. Elias decided that he was going and was taking me, our daughter Eve and Dean. Ed Miller was going along as well. We left early in the morning, and when we got home, the women in our house had everything all changed around. Plus, they had made a new rule because they disagreed with the way Elias and I made the rules about sitting at the table to eat breakfast, lunch, and supper. At my dad's house, we always fixed our plates and sat around wherever there was room. I didn't want that in my house, but now the women changed it. Elias agreed with the women and went against me, so I had no choice. To this day, I believe they did these things out of revenge because I went to the sale and they did not. They were also trying to separate me and Elias. The woman didn't like it that we sat beside each other at the table. Remember Millie was one of the women staying at my house. Troublemaker.

My dad found out that we got into a fight at my house, so he came over the next Monday and ordered Maggie and Millie up the hill to Maggie's house because he knew they were the fighters. Valerie went home, too. The only ones left were Leon, Ed Miller with his kids, and Mom. So easy and a huge relief! Now we can breathe.

First Cuttings

ANOTHER HORSE SALE WAS COMING up, and my brother Jonas came up with the idea that all the men and boys would go to the sale. The day came, and the men went to the sale. What most of us didn't know was what some of the men had planned for after the sale.

On the way home, the men asked their driver to stop at Bishop Ruben Hershberger's house. Bishop Ruben was the bishop who had made the final decision that it was okay to take away Lawrence Troyer's six-month ban without further punishment. He also supported Sheriff Frank Abrams taking Adam and Winnie's girls away from their mother and our community. So, as a way to send the message that we needed our little girls back, the men cut Bishop Ruben's hair and beard completely off.

From there, the men traveled to Bishop Malachi's home in Carrollton, Ohio. They planned to do the same thing to Malachi, but he met them at the door and did not invite them inside. A fight started right there in the yard. While the men did not cut hair, Jonas grabbed Malachi's beard and pulled out a big chunk. Malachi then grabbed Jonas's beard, and he lost a big chunk of his, too.

The Hershberger's called for the Holmes County police to come because they were horrified by the Bergholz Amish attack. Now questions and more questions were being asked like crazy. They requested proof of this and proof of that. Oh my, what a mess to clean up. Leon Miller, Jonas Mullet, and Larry Mullet were handcuffed and taken to the Holmes County jail. Later, the police came back and picked up Leroy Miller. Then they found out they got the wrong one and brought Leroy Miller back home. Delbert Mullet and Ed Miller turned themselves in because they were involved. The punishment of being sent to jail was meant to tell the men to not ever do such a thing again. My dad paid the bail to get everyone back home.

Life continued like normal for a bit with school, cooking, baking, chores, and the workers working as carpenters. Then one day the Millers decided to gang up and go to Geauga County. They planned to attack their parents the same way they did the others. Like the bishops, their parents had agreed with Adam Troyer and the taking of our community's little girls away by the sheriff. It was late at night when the Millers arrived in Geauga County. Leroy sort of hid his face with his hat and knocked on the door. As soon as the door opened, he walked in, dragged his dad out of bed, and shaved his head and beard off. Then he grabbed his mom and shaved her hair off as well.

To attack their parents after the men had already been sent once to the Holmes County jail was craziness. Now all could see that jail time did not scare the Bergholz community.

— 22 —

More Attacks

Soon after the Miller boys had attacked their parents, Leon, who had been living at our house for a while, decided to invite Douglas Wengard, one of his old buddies from Ashland, to visit. Leon's plan was to cut Douglas's hair and beard off because, after Douglas had found out that people were being put in coops to confess their sins, he kept calling the sheriff to search for Leon. Leon thought Douglas should stop being nosey and should mind his own business because Douglas had never cared or visited when Leon was still living in Ashland.

Douglas and his wife accepted Leon's invitation and came to visit on a Saturday. Leon told me not to serve coffee because he wanted to put ex-lax in Douglas's coffee. We figured Douglas should have known he would be attacked, considering all the things that had happened in our community, but he came into the house and sat in a rocking chair like nothing was going on.

Rejection

The rest of us kept looking at each other and smiling because he didn't have a clue what the plan was. I cooked a good dinner, and we all ate. Then Leon asked Douglas if he wanted to see the crops back in the fields. Douglas was willing to go, so I sat with his wife and visited until the men came back. Douglas was shaved clean and unhappy.

Not long afterward, Elias invited his parents to visit because it had been about five years since we had last seen them. He wrote a letter inviting them and promising them they would be safe. Then he told me to read the letter so that I knew about it. He signed both of our names on the letter even though I begged him not to sign mine because I didn't want to go to prison and leave my children alone. I knew that Elias planned to attack his dad, Martin Shrock, during the visit, and I knew we had been warned not to attack anyone else.

But Elias didn't listen to me because my dad had given him the orders. At this point in life, Elias would have done anything my dad asked because Elias had always been the outcast. He thought, if he listened to my dad, it would help him be accepted by the family. When the men sat in the circle to visit on Sunday, Wednesday, and Friday nights, Dad gave out orders for what he wanted everyone to accomplish. Then he'd join the women's circle and give the same orders. After the orders were given out to everyone, Dad would roll his chair out of the circle and say, "I want you to know I haven't told you to do anything. If you do this, it will be completely of your own free will." This is why the men and women always did their very best to say it was them and my dad had nothing to do with it. My Dad was innocent—it was our choice. And it was Elias's choice to obey my dad.

One evening, Martin and Arlene, Elias's parents, arrived behind Sheriff Frank in his police car with its lights blinking. Sheriff Frank parked and knocked on our door. Elias opened the door, and Sheriff Frank told us that he wanted to make sure Martin and his wife were going to be completely safe while they visited. Knowing plans had already been made, Elias promised Sheriff Frank that everything would be fine and nobody would get hurt.

I cooked supper for Martin and Arlene, but they didn't want to eat because trust had been lost when they were shunned from the Bergholz community. Plus, they were afraid we poisoned the food. Martin told us that, after Douglas was at our house, he got extremely sick on the way home, so they figured we had poisoned him. (It was only the ex-lax working.) So, Elias and I ate supper with the kids and visited afterward. Approximately two hours after supper, Martin said it was time for them to go home, and he thanked us for welcoming them and having a nice visit.

Then, Elias said, "I want to ask you one more thing before you leave, Dad. You always taught us as Amish people to stay away from the sheriff and not ask for their protection. Now, you, as our dad, have done that exact thing."

Martin replied that it wasn't him that had called the sheriff. Elias's brother had called for Dad and Mom to be protected because Elias's brothers did not trust Elias anymore.

Martin's answer wasn't good enough for Elias. He stood up

and went over to the drawers where he had hidden the scissors in preparation. He got the scissors out and said, "Well, maybe this will teach you a lesson to not call the sheriff." He then grabbed Martin and started cutting his hair.

Martin struggled to get away, but my older boys instantly stood up and helped Elias by holding Martin by the arm. When Martin saw that there was no chance in fighting back, he just stood there and allowed them to finish cutting his hair and beard. When Arlene saw what was going on, she started screaming for help and ran toward the door. Elias ordered me to grab her and not let her outside. Because Arlene put up a huge fight that was more than I could handle alone, Elias told Eve, our daughter, to help me hold her. All of this was part of Elias's plan to get me and the children involved on purpose. After everything was done, we talked a little and they left.

We were scared now because Sheriff Frank had told us not to cut hair or do anything stupid. As soon as they left, Elias, the children, and I all walked across the field to my dad's house to let him know the order was finished. Dad and all the women had a good laugh about it and thought it was very funny, but I was so scared I was shaking. We had been warned already to not continue with the beard cuttings, so I was sure we would all get arrested.

— 23 —

Arrest

NOTHING HAPPENED FOR A COUPLE of weeks until November 23, 2011. At six o'clock in the morning, our whole house and farm lit up with flashing bright lights. I knew it was Sheriff Frank, and I yelled loudly to wake the others up. Ed and his children and Leon Miller, who were all still living at our house, were upstairs sleeping. When I ran upstairs to wake them up, Ed told me to stay away from the front door. We could hear the police banging on the door and yelling for us. When I went back downstairs, Elias was walking toward the door. I yelled for him to come back. He turned around and went into our bedroom where he picked up three-year-old Jeremy and placed him on his lap. Elias and I sat together on our cedar chest with both bedroom doors closed.

We heard the police come inside, and Sheriff Frank opened our bedroom door. He told us he wanted Elias to come out, but Elias refused. Sheriff Frank entered the bedroom and took hold of Elias's arm. After I picked Jeremy up off Elias's lap, Sheriff Frank handcuffed Elias, took him to the kitchen, and made him sit in a chair. Next, Sheriff Frank went upstairs and handcuffed Ed and Leon. The other officers, mostly members of the Federal Bureau of Investigation, ordered the rest of us to follow in a line and sit on the couch so they could see everyone. Before they left, I was told they were going to take the men to Youngstown, Ohio, to meet a judge and they would let us know what was going on later in the day.

After the FBI and police left, I was alone with all my kids (except Mark and Eddie who were staying upstairs at my dad's shop) plus five of Ed Miller's children. At this point, the children were beside themselves because it was early in the morning and they had watched police arrest their father. Thirteen kids crying and crying. Before long, someone from Dad's house came over and told us that the authorities had taken Dad and my three brothers—Jonas, Larry, and Delbert. We were devastated.

A couple of days later, all of us women went with a van driver to search for the men. We knew they were in Youngstown, but we did not know where. We searched lots of different facilities but didn't find the right one until almost evening. They were at the CCA holding facilities in Youngstown. Because it was after visiting hours, we were not allowed to visit. The guards told us what hours to come back the next day and we did. After that first visit, we visited every week and took turns going in since there were a lot of us. This went on for a couple of weeks until the men went to trial and were found guilty.

The rest of us who were involved in the beard cuttings, including myself, were indicted and had to get a lawyer. Because most of us had young children, the court allowed us to stay home rather than go to jail while we arranged for our children's care. All together, sixteen of us—ten men and six women—were arrested or indicted. We faced a combined eighty-seven felony charges that included hate crimes, conspiracy, and obstructing justice charges, among others.

Weeks later, all of us plus our individual lawyers went to the federal court in Cleveland, Ohio, and stood in front of a judge. He allowed each of us to decide if we wanted a jury trial or twenty-five years to life in prison. Talk about being scared. I was shaking so badly. All I could think was I would be locked up and never able to be with my children ever again. Twenty-five years to life! We all chose to have a jury trial.

In August 2012, the trial began and lasted for over two weeks. We were in court every single day. While we waited on our verdict at the end of those weeks, a television played in the waiting room. We were Amish and not supposed to watch television, but Mervin decided to switch the channel to a western movie. In my mind, we had been trying to tell the world we weren't violent people, but when Mervin changed the channel to a western movie with shooting and we all sat there watching, we told the world exactly who we were.

Within five minutes of Mervin changing the channel, the verdict was in. Guilty. All of us were heading to federal prison. Each of our sentences was different because not all the counts

Rejection

were the same. I received two years while the five other women received one year. My sentence was longer because I was involved in two different incidents at my house. Even though I had nothing to do with the disagreements between Leon and his buddy and between Elias and his dad, I was charged with conspiracy because I was there. Dad received fifteen years, and the other men received anywhere from three to seven years. The judge said Dad received the longest sentence because he was the leader and he had the authority to stop us but didn't.

(To learn more about the trial and our sentencing, read the book written by Donald Kraybill. During the trial, he was called as an expert witness about Amish culture, traditions, and beliefs. The information in his book came from trial transcripts and interviews with Englishers and those who had left Bergholz. All of us involved were upset he wrote the book without our permission or talking to us. Plus, he was making money off people he didn't know. However, his book will fill in some gaps in my story if you want to know more.)

After the sentencing, each family had an adult left to take care of the children while the dad or mom went to federal prison. Except my family. Both Elias and I were sentenced to prison. Our ten children were old enough—the youngest was three years old and the oldest was twenty years old—to go on with everything, but it still wasn't right that our kids were left without parents.

The judge separated the sixteen of us to fourteen different facilities across the country. Amelia and I were sent to the federal women's facility in Waseca, Minnesota. On April 11, 2013, my lawyer drove Amelia and me, her husband, and my son Eddie to the Cleveland airport. We flew to Minnesota and stayed in a hotel overnight. The next day we said goodbye for now and walked into the federal facility. Amelia's husband and Eddie flew back home the next day. All the others were sentenced to facilities closer to home and could use a van driver to get to their facilities.

And so federal prison life began for all of us. Being inside those prison walls gave me the opportunity to change and never be the same person again. My next book, *Changed and Accepted*, will reveal those details.

To be continued ...

About the Author

Linda Shrock left the Amish of Bergholz, Ohio, in 2012 after leading a very dark, confusing life. She was married for twenty-seven years and has ten children. She was living a normal Amish life when some problems occurred and she ended up serving a two-year prison sentence in federal prison. Her time in prison changed her life completely. She was introduced to many other people and to church in prison where she found freedom and the Light of Jesus. She is now living a peaceful, quiet life in town with some of her children and attends Grace Point Ministry church. Through all her struggles, God has been so good to her.

Coming Soon!

Changed AND ACCEPTED

Linda Shrock

Look for *Changed and Accepted*
at your favorite online bookstores!